*Guillén
on
Guillén*

Guillén on Guillén

The Poetry and the Poet

TRANSLATED BY
Reginald Gibbons (POETRY)
Anthony L. Geist (COMMENTARY)

PRINCETON UNIVERSITY PRESS

Published by Princeton University Press, Princeton, New Jersey
In the United Kingdom: Princeton University Press, Guildford, Surrey

Library of Congress Cataloging in Publication Data will be
found on the last printed page of this book

Publication of this book has been aided by a grant from The Paul
Mellon Fund of Princeton University Press

This book has been composed in VIP Bembo

Clothbound editions of Princeton University Press books
are printed on acid-free paper, and binding materials are
chosen for strength and durability.

Printed in the United States of America by
Princeton University Press, Princeton, New Jersey

Table of Contents

The Morning of December 7, 1975

Notes and Appendices

« Obra completa »

Tanto verso, tanta copla
Va formando un solo río
Gracias a musa que sopla.
Se impone y rige: «Yo guío»...
«¿Musa torrencial?» No tanta.
Ningún Castillo de Otranto,
Pesadilla del magín.
La palabra rigurosa,
Tronco a tronco, rosa a rosa,
Crea el precioso jardín.

Jorge Guillén

Complete Works

So many verses, many rhymes
Have formed a single stream
Thanks to the muse who inspires.
She comes to take command: "I'll lead."
"A pouring, stormy muse?" Not so.
Here's no Castle of Otranto,
The Fancy in a nightmare's throes.
It is the rigorous word,
Trunk by trunk, rose by rose,
That creates the lovely garden.

Translators' Preface

When the Spanish government awarded the Miguel de Cervantes Prize for Literature to Jorge Guillén on December 1, 1976, it at last granted an official recognition to Spain's finest living poet. Guillén, of course, was famous before then, a poet who did not need "official" recognition. Since the 1950s he has received a number of prestigious literary awards in the United States and Europe. Indeed, he became an acknowledged master in the early twenties with the appearance of his first poems. But the Spanish award, coming so late, serves to commemorate the shape and importance of Guillén's entire work. At every stage his poetry has shown the careful, deliberate hand of a craftsman who would not be hurried into a poetic career, but who by his very meticulousness won himself a wide and admiring audience in the Spanish-speaking world. Each of the five volumes that followed *Cántico*, first published in 1928, has reaffirmed his reputation and won him more readers. Despite the difficulty of acquiring his works in Spain (for many years after the Civil War all his poetry was published abroad), Guillén has continued to exert great influence in his own country. Through the vicissitudes of two wars and—until recently—voluntary exile he has sustained the special poetic vision which imparts unity to "la Obra," his life's work.

During the years of Jorge Guillén's formation and maturity as an artist civil disorder and political strife wracked Spain. From the end of the Great War until the military uprising under Franco in 1936 severe labor unrest and economic depression aggravated the national crisis that culminated in the Civil War. While the nation declined politically, however, the arts flourished, as if detached from the surrounding turmoil. Guillén is one of a group of remarkably talented poets— among them Federico García Lorca, Rafael Alberti, Pedro Salinas, Luis Cernuda and Vicente Aleixandre (awarded the Nobel Prize for Poetry in 1977)—who wrote some of the finest poetry to appear in Spain since the "Golden Age" of the sixteenth and seventeenth centuries. Called "the Generation of 1927," from the year in which they gathered in Seville to commemorate the tricentenary of the death of Góngora, they formed not a "school" (as Guillén himself is quick to point out), but a poetic community. Bound by close ties of friendship and a shared belief in poetry, they published numerous literary magazines, gathered for frequent readings, and together lived their art intensely. They signed no manifestos; each maintained a distinct personality and poetic voice, yet they were united by a common vision of the world and of poetry's place in it.

"Dehumanization" and "pure poetry" were the aesthetic catchwords of the day. The phrase "dehumanization of art," coined by José Ortega y Gasset in his famous 1925 essay of that title, was widely used and abused during these years. Some more traditional critics took up the term and turned it against the Generation of 1927, denouncing their poetry as "cerebral" and bloodless. In their early years Guillén and his contemporaries did, in fact, strive to keep their poetry free of sentimentality, a quality they, like Valéry, considered the worst of obscenities.

"Pure poetry," a concept derived from Poe by the French Symbolist and post-Symbolist poets, had become the subject of a lively polemic in France that spilled over into Spanish literary circles. Its adherents held that pure poetry, derived from a mystical force within the poet, was a combination of sound and sense akin in its purity to music. Guillén, himself often called a "pure" poet, had this to say in 1926 about "la poésie pure": "Pure poetry is what is left in the poem after eliminating everything that is not poetry." Rather than accept the French doctrine without question, Guillén added, "I am decidedly in favor of compound, complex poetry, of the poem made of poetry and other human things. In sum, a 'somewhat pure poetry,' *ma non troppo*." While *Cántico* approaches this concept of purity more closely than does the work of Alberti, Lorca, or Cernuda, Guillén's verse is anything but "inhuman" or "pure," as we trust will be apparent to readers of this collection. It is precisely a human poetry, concerned with man's existence in the world, his relation to the objects around him.

Cántico remains Guillén's best known and most widely studied book. The work of a cosmopolitan yet supremely Castilian poet, it alone would be sufficient to assure Guillén a place of distinction in twentieth-century European letters. Yet he is in fact the author of three major books which represent a life-long devotion to his craft. Gathered together under the title *Aire nuestro*, they form a remarkable whole and present a coherent vision of creation and man's place in it. Guillén himself has likened his architectural scheme, in its unity, to Baudelaire's *Fleurs du mal* and Whitman's *Leaves of Grass*.

The complete version of *Cántico* forms the first part of *Aire nuestro*. Originally the work of Guillén's youth, *Cántico* took shape and grew through four successive editions over many years, from seventy-five poems in 1928 to three hundred thirty-four in 1950. The poems, carefully wrought and formally sophisticated, convey a sense of poetic and moral exploration. They are the response of a poet of unusual sensibility to those aspects of the world that seem to him to embody the qualities of coherence, vitality, equilibrium, and light. They present a decorous rapture, a song—"cántico"—of affirmation and wonder at creation.

After the publication of the definitive edition of *Cántico* in 1950, Guillén cast his net wider. The three books of *Clamor* followed, published originally over a span of several years. *Clamor* is a response to *Cántico* as well as an extension of the early work. Destruction, evil, and death form the dissonant chorus of *Clamor* that threatens to drown out the harmonies of *Cántico*. War, exile, and the loss of those close to the poet could not help being reflected in the spirit and work of a man as sensitive and aware of his surroundings as Guillén. Subtitled "Tiempo de historia," *Clamor* adds a historical dimension that complements the concern with the present, and with presences, that is essential to *Cántico*. If in this central volume

5

of *Aire nuestro* Guillén registers the discord of the world around him, he does not succumb to it. In the poems of *Clamor*, largely free verse meditations, the poet attempts, by an effort of will, to give form to worldly chaos in order to understand and contain it.

Homenaje, first published in 1967, concludes *Aire nuestro* and crowns the poetic labor of some fifty years. The record of Guillén's respect and admiration for other writers and works, his masters and touchstones, it is a kind of poetic daybook of Guillén's own formation. A remarkable consistency of tone and manner underlies *Aire nuestro*; its three parts strengthen and deepen the ethical and poetic vision announced in Guillén's earliest work. *Y otros poemas*, appearing in 1973 as a long epilogue to the trilogy, does not participate in the architectural shape of *Aire nuestro*, but extends the vision of the poet further.

The coherence of Guillén's work, on which he himself has insisted, has led some critics to mistake poetic consistency for "complacency." Seizing upon a line from "Beato sillón," one of the best known *décimas* in *Cántico*, "The world is well made," they have found Guillén's work lacking in a critical view of man. Guillén has countered this attack in prose and poetry, and has not found himself wanting for defenders. "From Contact to Act," a poem included in this anthology, answers for the poet: "The human world will never be well made."

The tone of serene contemplation in many of Guillén's poems results, in fact, from the effort of achieving a vital contact and interaction with the world, a sometimes hard-won meshing of observer and observed. Guillén's restrained fervor is never passive, for his work as a whole pursues a difficult goal: to embrace and comprehend all human activity. "Fe de vida," the subtitle that Guillén added to the 1945 edition of *Cántico*, could well serve to characterize all of *Aire nuestro*. More than just an expression of "faith in life," Guillén's poetry stands as a document of certification, a "verification of life." *Aire nuestro* bears witness to the complexity and inexhaustible variety of experience; it constitutes the poetic record of Guillén's encounters with the world—of which he feels himself a part.

The poetry of *Aire nuestro*, rooted in the poet's lifelong exploration of daily reality, often deals with familiar items of day-to-day living, such as the table and chair in "Perfectly Level," or

> El balcón, los cristales,
> Unos libros, la mesa.
> ¿Nada más esto? Sí,
> Maravillas concretas.
> (The balcony, windows,
> Some books, the table.
> Just this? Yes,
> Concrete wonders.)
> (*Cántico*, "Más allá," IV)

These humble objects do not stand simply for unmediated reality. To represent the real, Guillén must transform it, seeking the true nature of things about him, all the while never losing sight of their concrete, tangible surface. "Reality," Guillén has written, "not realism." The poet, then, sensitive to both appearances and essences, strives for the plenitude of a moment of consciousness fully open to the world around him. So much so, in fact, that Guillén will repudiate any sense of himself as the creator of the reality he takes into his poems. "La realidad me inventa," he says, "Reality invents me" (*Cántico*, 18). Everyday objects assume the greatest importance, therefore, in Guillén's poems. The poet's receptivity and craftsmanship disentangle these elements of the real world and set them apart, in exact relationship to one another and to the poet, so that they may express their full essence. In this way, they simultaneously maintain their common nature and rise above the ordinary.

We do not have to look far for analogues in other languages and other eras. Whether it be Coleridge's concrete universal, Eliot's objective correlative, or William Carlos Williams' mere things, this sense of poetry is not unfamiliar. The rigorous intellectual attention that Guillén brings to sensual experi-

7

ence, however, distinguishes him among modern poets. To some small degree it is the Spanish literary tradition that allows him to unite the humble table and the abstract notion of "reality" so gracefully and so immediately; but by the same token, the Anglo-American literary tradition may hinder the English-speaker's appreciation of Guillén's dexterity and seriousness in doing this.

Thus we do well to look to the formal texture of Guillén's poetry for the sense of physical presence which is so vital and impressive in his work. Guillén's mastery of exacting metrical forms, predominant especially in his early work, and his acute sense of formal effects at the most minute level of sound and sense, dignify those commonplace things and events that hold for him the values of vitality and coherence. He perceives experience as a kind of radiance of these values, and fixes them in poems whose metrical and musical shape expresses a contained ecstasy. If the phrase seems a paradox, let it then suggest the tension between form and matter characteristic of many poems in *Aire nuestro*. Yet Guillén's attention to form involves more than just the musical potential of the language. For him poetry serves a vital purpose. It must attempt to bring each moment to its plenitude, to draw order from chaos, to create, out of disorder, harmony:

> The sounds give me the sketch of flesh and bone.
> The life-preserving boon that saves me is the form.
> ("Toward the Poem")

Guillén achieves this particular effect, in a way his poetic signature, by various means. The elimination of the "anecdote"—the narrative element of a poem—leaves just an elliptical lyric essence. The five stanzas of "Nude," for example, present the stages of the poet's perception of a woman's body as he draws near her. The actual motion, however, the "situation," lies outside the poem. Even a poem as ostensibly narrative as "Setting Out" tells no story, but employs the *romance* form, traditional vehicle for narrative, as a kind of emblem itself of narration. It relates only the sensation of an action, filtered through a series of images abstracted from that action. The difficulty of Guillén's poetry, then, lies not in its apparent "obscurity" but in its clarity and precision.

Metaphor, which Guillén's generation, like their avant-garde predecessors, elevated to a position of supreme importance in their poetry, contributes in a special way to Guillén's work. His metaphors are not usually as stunning as Lorca's or Alberti's nor as ingenious as Salinas' or Gerardo Diego's, although in his early poems Guillén was not to be outdone by his contemporaries. By surprising imaginative twists and turns, the poets of the late twenties and early thirties sought to unlock the undreamed-of mystery in things; but Guillén's mature approach is at once more sober and more respectful of the reality he views. The essences and presences to which he pays homage draw the observer and the reader toward an almost Platonic sense of the ideal hidden within the real, yet the poems never fully break contact with the physical nor cease to delight in the sensual. This creates a special tension which, again, forms part of Guillén's poetic signature. He uses metaphor not to mystify the reader, but rather to assess the just proportions of precise observation. Though often a poet of things, he is also interested explicitly in ideas and emotions. His metaphors, then, frequently yoke not two disparate objects, but a level of emotional intensity with an essential perception: the woman in "Nude" is a "prodigious / Hoard of presence." In some of his later poetry Guillén can very nearly dispense with metaphor entirely, as in "On Television."

In general the vocabulary of *Aire nuestro* consists principally of nouns (either abstract—"reality," "plenitude," "clarity," —or concrete—"cradle, roses, balcony") with few qualifiers. Joaquín Casalduero, one of Guillén's first and most perceptive critics, wrote simply that in *Aire nuestro* "the exact placement of the word reveals its essential sense." So another kind of purity, this time of diction, lies at the center of Guillén's work, and his concern to penetrate to essential sensations determines the way in which many poems work with few verbs to arrive at an expansive moment of awareness, a state of rapture.

The book the reader has before him does not represent the Guillén of the anthology pieces, in new translation. Rather, through the poet's own selection and commentary, it is meant to suggest the essential unity of *Aire nuestro*, the stylistic, architectural and ethical coherence of his life's work.

The book came into being in unique circumstances. The translators had received Guillén's kind invitation to meet with him in Cambridge, Massachusetts. He greeted us at the door of the home of his daughter, where Guillén and his wife, doña Irene, live when not in Europe or California. He showed us to his study, a small room under the eaves of the house, lined with books that spill over onto the floor. Góngora peers sternly from one wall, as though watching over one who had rescued him from three centuries of vituperation. The facsimile of a Mallarmé poem in manuscript, found by Guillén's lifelong friend and fellow poet, Pedro Salinas, hangs on another wall. Guillén's desk faces a window, overlooking a tree-lined street. It was by pointing to that window, or rapping his knuckles on the desk, that Guillén would punctuate, in the following hours, his assertion of the need in poetry for a sense of the real.

We found that don Jorge had chosen from his extensive work some forty poems, which he proposed to read to us and comment upon. The whole would constitute the poet's anthology, a thematic selection representative of the essential unity of his entire work. (The reader will note, in addition, a number of poems that Guillén, in his comments, introduces by title only.) What we were to hear for the next two days was not just a distinguished poet's reading of his work, but the remarks of a critic whose skills, so evident in *Language and Poetry* and in his essays of the twenties and thirties, he now turned to his own poetry.

As Guillén read from a copy of *Aire nuestro* or the later *Y otros poemas*, one of us would find the next poem for him in another copy, so that in an hour's time ("the length of a class"—the limit he set for each session) he could read and talk as much as he liked. Reading softly but emphatically, Guillén would launch into comments almost before he had closed his lips on a poem's last syllables, weaving a nearly seamless whole. By the end we had taped, from three sessions, more than five hours of reading, commentary, and conversation. Although the conversation between tapings, when doña Irene joined us, was informal and lively, much that was anecdotal in Guillén's talk will not be found in this volume. Essentially a man of reserve and discretion, as he is a poet of contained euphoria and tempered anger, Guillén did not wish to combine the discussion of his poetry with the relation of incidental asides. Animated, solicitous, attentive, and proud, he himself seemed to register a bit of awe as he contemplated the work of his pen over the years. His excitement when reading was genuine and moving, for he seemed to read his poems as if they were not only his own, but also a part of the world's work—the poetic body that accompanies individual and social history as a kind of numinous cloud around persons, events, incongruities, and triumphs.

We later transcribed the tapes and Guillén then edited them for this volume, shifting from the first-person to the third-person voice he has preferred in his published remarks about his own poetry. It should be recalled in reading the selection and commentary that, for the occasion of this book, Guillén asks us to consider first of all the total architecture of his work, not necessarily the progress from the first poems of *Cántico* to *Y otros poemas*. He does not wish to emphasize his development as a poet, but the coherence of his work as a whole. Thus the anthology proceeds not chronologically, but thematically, skipping back and forth to draw poems from every part of Guillén's work.

It would be impossible here to describe adequately the impression that don Jorge made on us. How can one capture the full measure of the spontaneity and emotion of his reading, the profound modesty and candor of his comments, the *plenitude*, to use one of his favorite words, of this poet passing in review the result of half a century's passionate devotion to his art, isolating in a few poems the essence of "la Obra"? Guillén has written some of the most important and beautiful poetry in Spanish. His characteristic poetic voice, which speaks with the same intonation and fervor from first poem to last, must necessarily grow fainter in translation. We, as translators, can only hope that some of Guillén's vitality and enthusiasm, as well as the strength and clarity of his work, has been preserved in this book.

ANTHONY L. GEIST
San Antonio de Béxar, Texas

REGINALD GIBBONS
Silverton, Devon, England

Mañana del 6 de diciembre de 1975

The Morning of December 6, 1975

La ordenación de esta antología manifiesta el conjunto unitario de la obra, *Aire Nuestro*, y su sentido coherente. Empezará casi con el nacimiento y terminará con la muerte. Se trata, pues, de una especie de trayectoria, que pondrá de relieve la composición de todo un conjunto y su esencial sentido constante.

Por supuesto, poemas que andan ya por las antologías quedarán eliminados. Por ejemplo, «Beato sillón», que fue muy mal entendido. «El mundo está bien hecho» se dice en esa décima. Bien hecho por Dios: la Creación. Lectores mal hechos, torpemente politizados, creyeron que el poeta alude a este mundo—tan corrupto—en que vivimos. La obra entera, *Aire Nuestro*, niega esa estúpida interpretación.

Comencemos con el primer poema de la obra: «Mientras el aire es nuestro». Introducción a la obra total. Se suele repetir que este poeta es el autor de un solo libro: *Cántico*. En realidad hay una sola obra compuesta de cuatro volúmenes: *Cántico*, *Clamor*, *Homenaje*, *Y Otros Poemas*. Al autor le importa mucho ese bloque unitario con su coherencia significativa: labor de unos cincuenta y cinco años. En suma: unas dos mil doscientas páginas. (Los amigos más exquisitos del autor no se lo perdonan . . .) *Cántico*, *Clamor*, *Homenaje* forman la trinidad de *Aire Nuestro* en su primera edición: tres, número dantesco. El autor siguió activo, y acogiéndose a la tradición inglesa—«And Other Poems»—compuso un volumen final, que tal vez, quién sabe, no será el último: *Y Otros Poemas*, estricta continuación simultánea de los tres primeros libros.

This anthology is organized in such a way as to show the underlying unity of the work, *Aire Nuestro (Our Air)*, and its coherent meaning. It begins almost with birth and ends with death. It is, then, a kind of trajectory, which points up its composition as a whole, and at the same time, a constant essential meaning.

Poems already published in other anthologies, of course, will be excluded from this one. "Beato sillón" ("Blessed Armchair"), for example, which has been seriously misunderstood. "The world is well made" it says in that *décima*.[1] Well made by God: Creation. Ill-formed readers, clumsily political, thought the poet was alluding to this corrupt world in which we live. The whole of *Aire Nuestro* denies such a stupid interpretation.

Let us begin with the first poem of the work: "While the Air is Ours." An introduction to the entire work. It is often said that this poet is the author of only one book: *Cántico*. In fact, there is but a single work, composed of four volumes: *Cántico, Clamor, Homenaje, Y Otros Poemas*. The coherence of meaning of this unified whole is of great importance to its author: the labor of some fifty-five years. A total of some two thousand two hundred pages. (The author's more exquisite friends will never forgive him. . . .) *Cántico, Clamor, Homenaje* form the trinity of *Aire Nuestro* in its first edition: Three, Dante's number. The author continued to write, and following the English tradition—"And Other Poems"— composed a final volume, which (who knows?) may not be the last: *Y Otros Poemas*, strictly and simultaneously a continuation of the first three books.

Aire Nuestro. Primer poema. «Mientras el aire es nuestro». El aire es el elemento fundamental en estas poesías. Elsa Dehennin, valiosa hispanista belga, descubrió con su «computer», que en *Cántico* las palabras más frecuentes son las relativas a la luz. («Une poésie de la clarté» llama a su estudio.) Sin embargo, es aún más esencial el aire. Por el aire establecemos nuestra relación con el mundo. Único tema de toda esta tentativa poética es la relación del hombre con esos alrededores. ¿No será tal vez el argumento capital de la literatura? Importa más el mundo que el sujeto. Aquí no se retrae hacia la vida interior. En otro poema se dice: «El mundo es más que yo». De ahí la importancia de la acción respiratoria.

Aire Nuestro. First poem. "While the Air is Ours." Air is the fundamental element in these poems. Elsa Dehennin, the excellent Belgian Hispanist, found with her computer that in *Cántico* the most frequent words are those that refer to light. ("Une poésie de la clarté" she calls her study.) Nevertheless, air is even more essential. Through air we establish our relationship with the world. The sole theme of this entire poetic endeavor is man's relationship with his surroundings. Isn't that perhaps the main theme of all literature? The world is more important than the subject. Here there is no retreat to the inner life. Another poem says: "The world is greater than I." Hence the importance of the act of breathing.

Mientras el aire es nuestro

Respiro,
Y el aire en mis pulmones
Ya es saber, ya es amor, ya es alegría,
Alegría entrañada
Que no se me revela
Sino como un apego
Jamás interrumpido
—De tan elemental—
A la gran sucesión de los instantes
En que voy respirando,
Abrazándome a un poco
De la aireada claridad enorme.

Vivir, vivir, raptar—de vida a ritmo—
Todo este mundo que me exhibe el aire,
Ese—Dios sabe cómo—preexistente
Más allá
Que a la meseta de los tiempos alza
Sus dones para mí porque respiro,
Respiro instante a instante,
En contacto acertado
Con esa realidad que me sostiene,
Me encumbra,
Y a través de estupendos equilibrios
Me supera, me asombra, se me impone.

While the Air is Ours

I breathe
And the air in my lungs
Is knowledge now, and love, and joy,
An embodied joy
That reveals itself to me
Only as a cleaving—
So elemental
That it never breaks off—
To the great succession of instants
In which I continue to breathe,
Embracing a part
Of the enormous airy clarity.

To live, to live, to seize from the rhythm of life
All this world that the air displays
And—God knows how—that pre-existing
Beyond
Which raises its gifts to the plateau of the ages
For me because I breathe,
I breathe from moment to moment,
In perfect contact
With that reality which sustains me,
Lifts me up
And through stupendous equilibria
Leaves me overcome, astonished, obedient.

Hay muchos hombres que se creen más importantes que todo lo demás. ¡No, no! Este «yo» es una parte minúscula de ese universo enorme. Habrá siempre que evitar la *hinchazón* del yo. Lo que debe prevalecer es la *inserción* en *ese* universo.

Sigamos adelante. Hay poemas sobre el niño. (Uno, largo, sobre el niño en la cuna: «El Infante».) Hay otro nacimiento diario: el despertar de cada mañana. Por eso hay tantos poemas sobre el despertar y sobre el amanecer, despertar del día. Leamos ahora otros versos que se refieren también a esa conexión primordial: «Del contacto al acto». No se alude sólo al simple contacto visual, sonoro, táctil. En seguida se produce una acción. Acción que no omite el pensamiento. Esta acción no es irracional. Nuestro contacto incluye una serie de acciones vitales, que implican sentimientos, intuiciones, decisiones, instintos—con su arrastre intelectual.

Many men think themselves more important than everything else. No, no! This "I" is a miniscule part of the enormous universe. One must always avoid *inflating* the ego. What must prevail is the act of *insertion* into *that* universe out there.

Let's move on. There are poems about children. (One, quite long—about a child in the cradle: "El Infante" ["The Infant"].) There is another daily birth: awaking each morning. That is why there are so many poems about awakening and dawn, the waking of the day [in *Cántico*]. Let us now read another poem that also refers to that primordial connection: "From Contact to Act." This does not just allude to mere visual, sonorous or tactile contact. It must immediately produce an action. Action that does not exclude thought. This action is not irrational. Our contact includes a series of vital actions, which imply feelings, intuitions, decisions, instincts—with all their intellectual implications as well.

Del contacto al acto

¿«Conformismo»? Jamás conforme estuve
Con esa imposición desordenada
Que es siempre el Orden. ¡Ah, la sociedad!
Nunca estará bien hecho el mundo humano.

Humanas criaturas hay capaces
De residir en esencial acorde,
Y por eso tan físico, tan denso,
Con esa realidad ahí surgida.

No se fracasa por deber diario.
Vivir no es cultivar una impotencia.
Varón será quien ame poseyendo.

—¿Acorde?—Poderío suficiente
Para asir esta vida, nuestra vida,
Y lograr el contacto fecundante.

From Contact to Act

"Conformism"? I was never to conform
To the disordered imposition
That Order always is. Ah—society!
The human world will never be well made.

But there are human creatures capable
Of living in an essential harmony
(And therefore one so physical, so rich)
With that reality, that burgeoning realm.

One does not fail because of daily duties.
To live is not to affect impotence.
A man is one whose love is a possessing.

And harmony?—Dominion will suffice
To grasp this life, our life, and thus achieve
The contact that is always fecund.

Se advierte, ¿verdad?, el esfuerzo, un esfuerzo de inteligencia y de alma, y también físico. Después vendrá el desenlace: el éxito o el fracaso. Pero ese esfuerzo apunta la tendencia a dominar la situación. Dominio personal del hombre, no poder social. Hay que entrar en el mundo y no quedarse fuera, o no quedarse derrotado, o peor—como algún exquisito: ser un derrotado de nacimiento.

Leamos una página sobre esa salida al mundo. Es un romance en una sola cláusula desde el principio hasta el fin, lo que favorece la impresión de impulso y movimiento. Un impulso—«¡Salir, salir . . .»—mueve toda la poesía. Se arroja al mar un hombre y se baña con sensación de frescura, luz, deporte, embriaguez, deleite de estar dominando ese momento marino.

You notice, of course, the effort, an effort as much intellectual and spiritual, as physical. Later will come the denouement: success or failure. But this effort points toward a tendency to dominate the situation. Man's personal domination, not social power. One must enter into the world and not remain outside it, nor be defeated by it, or what's worse—like some over-exquisite sorts—defeated from birth.

Let's read a page about going out into the world. It is a romance[2] written in a single sentence from beginning to end; this reinforces an impression of impulse and motion. A single impulse—"setting out"—moves the whole poem. A man dives into the sea and swims with a sensation of freshness, light, sport, intoxication, pleasure at dominating that moment of contact with the sea.

La salida

¡Salir por fin, salir
A glorias, a rocíos,
—Certera ya la espera,
Ya fatales los ímpetus—
Resbalar sobre el fresco
Dorado del estío
—¡Gracias!—hasta oponer
A las ondas el tino
Gozoso de los músculos
Súbitos del instinto,
Lanzar, lanzar sin miedo
Los lujos y los gritos
A través de la aurora
Central de un paraíso,
Ahogarse en plenitud
Y renacer clarísimo,
—Rachas de espacios vírgenes,
Acordes inauditos—
Feliz, veloz, astral,
Ligero y sin amigo!

Setting Out

To leave at last, to brilliant
Sea-spray and hosannahs—
With a knowing expectancy,
Irrevocable impulse—
To glide through the golden air
Of summer—Give thanks!—and then
To set the joyful skill
Of muscles—in a sudden
Access of instinct—against
The waves; and fearlessly,
Fearlessly to fling
All luxuries and cries
Across the central dawn
Of a paradise, to drown
In a plenitude and be
Reborn, utterly clear—
Gusts from virgin spaces,
Unheard-of harmonies—
Happy, speedy, astral,
Nimble, and alone!

De aquel hombre, resbalando «sobre el fresco / Dorado del estío» prorrumpe una exclamación: «¡Gracias!» por un sentimiento de gratitud. Esa acción de gracias es esencialmente *Cántico*. Y todo ello ocurre en una perspectiva de estío, la estación más adecuada para insertarse en el mar, en la Naturaleza. Y luego, «los músculos . . . del instinto», y los gritos de exaltación. Esta exaltación no es el único nivel de *Cántico*. Otras muchas veces se aspira a la serenidad, al equilibrio tenso, porque el equilibrio es una tensión. Este pasaje es más agitado. Hasta se dice «paraíso», siempre en hipérbole. Este poeta no busca paraíso, ni el de antes ni el final. La palabra no significa más que tránsito de dominación dichosa. Un poema se titula: «Jardín en medio». ¿En medio de qué? De todo lo que no es jardín: «El discorde mundo en torno». Y, pese a esas discordancias, «paraíso». Y «algún hombre / Con su minuto sereno». ¿Quién no ha sentido en su contacto con el mar ese «ahogarse en plenitud», una plenitud de Naturaleza primordial, de espacios vírgenes en toda su frescura y con sensación de velocidad, concentrada en los tres adjetivos bisílabos, oxítonos: «Feliz, veloz, astral»? Astral, por hipérbole, como un astro. «Ligero y sin amigos», ya como un cuerpo autónomo, que está dominando.

En otras ocasiones el tono es muy diferente. El poema «A nivel» pertenece a la tercera parte de *Clamor*: «A la altura de las circunstancias». Aquí se propone la relación de un señor con una mesa; una mesa cualquiera, dentro de una vida cotidiana.

That man, gliding "through the golden air of summer" exclaims out of a feeling of gratitude: "Give thanks!" *Cántico* is essentially that giving of thanks. And it all takes place in the context of summer, the best season for plunging into the sea, into Nature. And then, "muscles—in a sudden / Access of instinct," and the cries of excitement. This exultation is not the only level of *Cántico*. At other times it aspires to serenity, to a tense equilibrium, because equilibrium is a kind of tension. But this passage is more excited. It even mentions "paradise," though always as a hyperbole. The poet does not search for paradise, either before or after death. The word means no more than a transport of joyous domination. There is another poem, entitled "Jardín en medio" ("Garden in the Midst"). In the midst of what? Of everything that is not garden: "The discordant world about it." And, in spite of that discord, "paradise." And "A man / with his quiet moment." Who has not felt in his contact with the sea what it is like "to drown / In a plenitude," a plenitude of primordial Nature, of virgin spaces in all their freshness; and the sensation of speed, concentrated in three bi-syllabic, oxytonic adjectives: "Feliz, veloz, astral"? Astral, by hyperbole, like a star. "Nimble and alone," like an autonomous body now, in the act of domination.

At other times the tone is quite different. The poem "Perfectly Level" belongs to the third part of *Clamor*: "At the Height of Circumstances." This poem expresses the relation between a man and a table; any table, in an everyday life.

A nivel

Fácil no fue regir mis relaciones
De amistad con la mesa aquí presente
Desde esta silla en que la afronto ahora.
Se interpuso el trabajo apresurado,
Y una dolencia me indispuso en contra
De todo alrededor, jamás amable
Sin ojos ya serenos.
                              Es fatal:
Por entre muchos roces, circunstancias
—De muy varios niveles—nos exigen
Esfuerzo . . . de dominio.
                                        Silla, mesa,
En situación tranquila de acomodo
Con este al fin sosiego más que práctico,
Mantienen la virtud de un equilibrio
Donde figuro yo como energía
Necesaria.
                    Soy yo quien siente ahora
La paz triunfante aquí porque la oigo
Sin querer con mi oído y la acreciento
Con mi serenidad, fortalecida
Por esta justa posición de aplomo:
Yo y la tersa madera de esa mesa,
A un preciso nivel de circunstancia.

Perfectly Level

It was not easy to conduct my friendly
Relations with this table, from this chair
In which I face it now. My work—
In need of hasty doing—intervened,
Or an illness left me indisposed to all
The things around me, none of which seemed pleasing
When my eyes were not already calm.
                                        It's fate:
But the world rubs against us all day long,
And circumstances—of very different levels—
Require an effort . . . of dominion.
                                        This chair
And table, in the tranquil situation
Of their adjustment to a quiet more
Than merely practical, at last, maintain
The tense strength of an equilibrium
In which it's I who take the part
Of the needed energy.
                                        And I who feel
The triumphant peace here now, because I hear it,
Without even trying, in my own ears, and I
Widen it with my calm, strengthened by this
Judicious attitude of true-plumbed prudence:
Both I and the smooth wood of the table,
At a precise level of circumstance.

Esta poesía se acomoda al título «A la altura de las circunstancias». Prevalece la serenidad. Por eso viene bien aquí el endecasílabo sin rima. Se parte de una situación: algún pequeño conflicto: «el trabajo apresurado», «una dolencia». Esos «roces» exigen «Esfuerzo . . . de dominio» para conseguir el necesario acorde con la circunstancia. De ahí, los «ojos ya serenos». Se quiere una especie de *equilibrio*, término que no debe aquí llamarse clásico, sí término vital. No se piensa ahora en el maravilloso equilibrio griego. ¡No tanto! Sólo el equilibrio para vivir—en contacto y roce con el mundo, «a un preciso nivel de circunstancia».

El contacto puede ser más placentero. «Paraíso regado»: una décima. Es una estrofa que reaparece a través de todo *Aire Nuestro*. Lo redondo está compensado por lo flexible, con sus pausas y encabalgamientos. La distribución de las rimas sigue el modelo de la décima francesa. Pero es siempre la misma estrofa con toda su redondez.

This poem fits the title "At the Height of Circumstances." Serenity prevails. That is why the unrhymed hendecasyllable is appropriate here. It begins with a situation: some small conflict: "work / In need of hasty doing," "an illness." But the world that "rubs against us" requires an "effort . . . of dominion" to strike the necessary accord with circumstances. Hence, "eyes . . . already calm." One needs a sort of *equilibrium*, a term which here should not be called classical, but rather vital. Not the marvellous Greek equilibrium. Not that perfect! Just the equilibrium necessary to live—in contact and friction with the world. "At a precise level of circumstance."

The contact can be more pleasurable, as well. "An Irrigated Paradise": a *décima*. This is a stanzaic form that reappears throughout *Aire Nuestro*. The flexibility of the *décima*, with its pauses and enjambement, compensates for the roundness of the form. The distribution of rhymes follows the model of the French *décima*. But it is always the same stanza with all its roundness.

Paraíso regado

Sacude el agua a la hoja
Con un chorro de rumor,
Alumbra el verde y lo moja
Dentro de un fulgor. ¡Qué olor
A brusca tierra inmediata!
Así me arroja y me ata
Lo tan soleadamente
Despejado a este retiro
Fresquísimo que respiro
Con mi Adán más inocente.

An Irrigated Paradise

The water shakes the leaf
With a jet of sound,
Illumines the green, which steeps
In radiance. What a scent
Of rough, immediate earth!
So, by a cloudless firmament
Am I thrown here, and bound
To this retreat, where I retire
To breathe pure air, to conspire
With my Adam most innocent.

En suma: jardín. La luz atraviesa el chorro del agua que va regando ese paraíso. Y se funden el olor, la claridad, la sensación de lo inmediato, el placer en un «retiro fresquísimo» para quien se nombra Adán: el inocente gozador de la Naturaleza. (Quien no es Adán es el que compone la décima.)

Esto nos lleva a otro aspecto: el presente, capital enfoque en toda la obra. No el tiempo presente que algunos críticos denominan «intemporal», noción incomprensible para este poeta. El presente no está nunca suelto: posee pasado y va hacia el futuro «casi en movimiento». Algo inminente asoma, y esa inminencia arrastra porvenir. He ahí, en *Homenaje*, «Al margen de Las Mil y Una Noches». Se rememora aquella palabra en aquella historia de Aladino: «Sésamo». Un personaje de aventura llega a un palacio en el minuto que precede a una solemnidad.

That is: garden. Light pierces the jet of water that irrigates this paradise. And the smell, the clarity, the sensation of the immediate, the pleasure of "this retreat," all blend together for the one called Adam, who innocently enjoys Nature. (He who is not Adam is the author of this *décima*.)

This brings us to another aspect: the present, a capital focal point of the entire work. Not that present time which some critics call "timeless," a notion incomprehensible to this poet. The present is never free: it has a past and goes toward a future, "almost in motion." Something imminent appears, and that imminence bears with it a future. Thus we have, in *Homenaje*, "In the Margin of *The Thousand and One Nights*." "Sesame," that word from the story of Aladdin, comes to mind. An adventurer arrives at a palace the moment before a solemn act is to take place.

La inminencia

. . . Entonces dije: «Sésamo». La puerta
Con suavidad solemne y clandestina
Se abrió. Yo me sentí sobrecogido,
Pero sin embarazo penetré.

Alguien me sostenía desde dentro
Del corazón. De un golpe vi una sala.
Arañas por cristal resplandecían
Sobre una fiesta aún sin personajes.

Entre espejos, tapices y pinturas
Yo estaba solo. Resplandor vacío
Se reservaba al muy predestinado.

Y me lancé a la luz y a su silencio,
Latentes de una gloria ya madura
Bajo mi firme decisión. Entonces . . .

The Imminence

. . . Then I said *Sesame*. The door,
With solemn and clandestine ease,
Swung open. I was seized with fear
But nothing stopped me so in I went.

Someone bore me up inside
My heart. At a stroke I saw a room—
Through crystal chandeliers the light
Shone on an unattended feast.

Paintings, mirrors, tapestries—
I was alone, in an empty splendor
Reserved for one predestined here.

With that I threw myself into
The brilliant silence, a latent ripe
Magnificence at my resolve. And then . . .

«Entonces». Hay siempre una llamada a la voluntad. Lo de menos son «Las Mil y Una Noches». Importa la impresión de inminencia.

Ese paso hacia adelante no se da si no se siente esperanza. Cuando se pierda la esperanza por un camino se está muerto en la dirección de ese camino. Vida es inseparable de esperanza. Alguien diría: ¡Qué optimismo! No. Este autor detesta el término «optimismo». «Optimismo» y «pesimismo», ausentes del vocabulario de *Aire Nuestro*, constituyen teorías, opiniones. No son acción vital. Este sentimiento de esperanza es tan elemental como el aire en los pulmones. He aquí el poema «Vida-Esperanza», romance, sin cesar también movimiento.

"Then." There is always a call to the will. *The Thousand and One Nights* is the least of it. What matters is the impression of imminence.

This step forward cannot be taken if one doesn't have hope. To lose hope in a given path is to die in that direction. Life is inseparable from hope. Someone might say: What optimism! No. This author detests the term "optimism." "Optimism," "pessimism"—absent from the vocabulary of *Aire Nuestro*—are theories, opinions. They are not vital action. But the feeling of hope is as elemental as the air we breathe. Here is the poem "Life-Hope;" a *romance*, ceaseless motion also.

Vida-esperanza

Helo, por fin, bien despierto
Frente a frente a la jornada,
Que se extiende por un aire
Pronto a entregar la mañana
Siempre ignota, nunca neutra,
Turbia tal vez o entreclara,
Pero sin cesar atmósfera
Que los pulmones y el alma
Respiran sin distinguir
Entre el aire y la sustancia
Por él difusa, visible
Bajo forma de esperanza.
El despierto respirando
En su interior la derrama
De modo tan natural
Que no sabe de ella nada,
Y sólo vivir consigue
Mientras de un instante pasa
Mal o bien al otro instante,
Y algo ya inminente aguarda
Dispuesto a ser realidad
Que se incorpore a la gana
Tan continua de una vida
Sólo vida en su esperanza.

Life-Hope

Awake at last, he stands
Face to face with the day,
Which reaches through an air
Quick to offer him
The morning: always unknown,
Never neutral, perhaps
Murky or only half-
Clear but—ceaselessly—
An atmosphere that lungs
And soul breathe without
Distinguishing between
The air and that substance
Diffused in it that is
Visible in the form
Of hope. The wakened man
Who breathes so overflows
Inside himself with this
By nature that he knows
Nothing of it at all
And merely manages
To live, while moving from
One instant to the next,
For good or ill, and now
Awaits an imminent
Something disposed to be
Reality that will
Incorporate itself
To the constant desire
Of a life that is life
Only out of hope.

¿Está claro? El poeta padece la mala fama de ser oscuro. ¡No tanto! Si se reúnen unas poesías con otras resalta una continuidad que viene de dentro, no de fuera. Esa esperanza ¿qué encontrará? Por de pronto, eso que está ahí: el vivir de todos los días, el desarrollo cotidiano. Lo que disgustará a quien identifique poesía y belleza. No incurramos en ese burdo error. La poesía está en el poema, no en la realidad hermosa. Esta mesa no es pictórica. Pictórica lo será en una pintura. Nada tiene que ver lo cotidiano con elementos feos, neutros, hostiles—sin relación con la hermosura, prejuicio del romántico, del esteta, que tropezaban en esa zona real y en sus representaciones como si fuesen negativas. El tejido de la vida se nos entrega formado por su minúscula continuidad. Lo resume un breve poema: «Media mañana». Leamos ahora el romance.

Is that clear? This poet has the bad reputation of being obscure. It's not all that obscure! If you put some poems alongside others, a continuity becomes apparent that comes from within, not from without. And that hope, what will it find? First of all, all that out there: day-to-day living, the daily routine. Which will displease those who identify poetry and beauty. Let's not fall into that gross error. The poetry is in the poem, not in some beautiful reality. This table is not pictorial. It will be so in a painting. Daily life has nothing to do with some ugly, neutral, or hostile elements, incompatible with beauty. That is a prejudice of the romantic and the aesthete, who stumble in the zone of reality and over its representations as though they were negative. The fabric of life is given to us formed by the continuity of all its minute parts. This is summarized in a short poem: "Media mañana" ("Mid-morning"). But let's read the *romance*.

Vida cotidiana

¡Vida sin cesar cotidiana!
Así lo eres por fortuna,
Y entre un renacer y un morir
Día a día te das y alumbras
Lunes, martes, miércoles, jueves
Y viernes y . . .
        Todos ayudan
A quien va a través de las horas
Problemáticas pero juntas
En continuidad de rosario.
¡Dominio precario!
        Se lucha
Por asentar los pies en Tierra,
Por ser punto real de la curva
Que hacia los espacios arrastra
Nuestra ambición de criaturas,
Anhelantes de hallar contacto
Con los relieves, las arrugas
De la realidad inmediata,
Por eso difícil y dura,
Dura de su propio vigor,
Que mis manos al fin subyugan
De costumbre en costumbre.
        ¡Vida
Tan cotidiana! Sin disculpa.

Everyday Life

This never-ending everyday life!
It is your luck to be this way,
And between being born and dying
Day by day you give yourself—you illumine—
Monday, Tuesday, Wednesday, Thursday,
Friday. . . .
         They all abet
The one who threads his way through hours
That are problematic yet
Continuous, linked like a rosary.
Precarious dominion!
         One fights
To set one's feet upon the earth,
To be the real point on the curve
That draws our creaturely ambition
Toward distant spaces,
Where we want to touch
All rippling surfaces, the wrinkles
Of an immediate reality,
One therefore difficult and harsh
(Harsh from its own strength)
Which my two hands subdue at last
From habit to habit.
         A life
So everyday! Without apology.

Este «Sin disculpa» ya es polémico. ¡Esos estetas! Poesía en romance, y la sucesión de la asonancia, única en todo el poema, conviene al hilo cotidiano. (No hay distribución en estrofas.) Todo ello implica lo de «¡Dominio precario!». El vivir, día por día, es difícil y no precisamente seguro. Lo bueno, lo malo, lo positivo, lo negativo se hallan juntos y hasta simultáneamente. O sea: «Jardín en medio», la realidad tal cual es. Acudamos a otra página: «Castillo de Elsinor».

Recuerdos de Italia y de Hamlet se funden en ese insomnio. Aquel castillo—italiano, danés—hacía pensar en historias elevadas, en el amor. El rayo de luna sobre una almena era como el anillo amoroso. Y de repente—otro recuerdo—aparecía una rata. Y de esta oposición surge el sentido del poema. Todo va junto: los «príncipes errantes sin consuelo», la «luz de arriba» con tragedia, con rey. «Y la rata cruzó por luz de arriba». En el insomnio, en la conciencia despierta se ofrece todo a la vez y su contraste.

This "without apology" is, of course, polemical. Those aesthetes! The *romance* meter, and the continuation of assonance, maintained throughout the poem, is appropriate to the thread of daily life. (The poem is all one stanza.) All of this implies a "Precarious dominion!" Living, day to day, is difficult and by no means a sure thing. Good and bad, positive and negative, exist together, and even simultaneously. That is: "Garden in the midst," reality just as it is. Let's turn to another page: "Elsinore."

Memories of Italy and of Hamlet join in this state of insomnia. That castle—Italian or Danish—provoked thoughts of lofty subjects, of love. Moonlight around a tower was like the finger in a wedding ring. And suddenly—another memory—a rat appeared. The meaning of the poem arises from this opposition. It all goes together: the "errant princes inconsolably sad," the "light from above" with tragedy, with a king. "And the rat scuttered through the light from above." In this insomnia, in this wakeful awareness, everything and its opposite appears as one.

Castillo de Elsinor

(Insomnio)

Yo no veía ningún alma en pena
Vagar ante los muros del castillo.
De pronto percibí desliz de brillo:
Rata alumbrada se asoció a mi escena.

La luna prefería cierta almena,
Y un rayo era ya el dedo en el anillo
Del amor tan audaz y tan sencillo
Que a un oro del futuro se encadena.

Sin historia la rata, primitiva,
Me condujo a un pasado con sus duendes,
Sus príncipes errantes sin consuelo.

Y la rata cruzó por luz de arriba,
De tragedia, de rey. Tú sí me entiendes,
Luna. Todo convive en mi desvelo.

Elsinore

(Insomnia)

I saw no soul in torment roving round
The castle walls. Then I perceived a slight
Glittering movement as a rat that joined
My scene ran through a bar of light.

The moon preferred some battlements, one ray
Became the finger in the ring
Of a love so brave, of such simplicity,
That to the future's gold it bound its link.

That rat, pastless and primitive,
Led me back to a time with ghosts,
With errant princes inconsolably sad.

And the rat scuttered through the light from above,
From tragedy and kings. You understand
Me well, moon: in my watch, all coexists.

Continuemos avanzando con el protagonista de esas aventuras, que no es precisamente la persona que escribe. Responsable de todo ello es el autor. Pero ese protagonista es ya otro personaje—que pertenece al mundillo creado en el poema. La tan conocida frase de Rimbaud es muy justa: « 'je' est un autre». Pues bien, este personaje siente una propensión afirmativa: «porque es mi sino / Propender con fervor al universo»—nos asegura en otro poema (*Cántico*, «Además»). Esta propensión llega hasta el sumo acuerdo: el amor. Amor: tema capital de estas poesías. Entre las numerosas páginas amorosas, ¿cuál escoger ahora para ser leída en alta voz? Comencemos, a manera de prólogo, por «Desnudo». Mi amigo el profesor Edmund L. King me contaba cómo explicaba este poema a sus alumnos: «Vayan ustedes entrando en la habitación lentamente, y allí, en el fondo, se verá a una mujer; y puede ser en el verano, y todo está en sosiego. Y se desemboca en una contemplación serena».

Let us move on with the protagonist of these adventures, who is not precisely the writer. The author is responsible for it all. But that protagonist is a different character now—who belongs to the little world created in the poem. Rimbaud's well-known phrase is quite appropriate: " 'je' est un autre." Fine then, this character feels a tendency toward affirmation: "because it is my fate / To lean fervently toward the universe" —he assures us in another poem (*Cántico*, "Además"). This tendency strikes the ultimate accord: love. Love: a major theme of this poetry. Among all the love poems, which one should we choose to read now? Let's begin, as a kind of prologue, with "Nude." My friend Professor Edmund L. King told me how he explained this poem to his students: "You enter slowly, and there, at the far end of the room, you see a woman; it might be summer, and everything is at rest. And it all leads to serene contemplation."

Desnudo

Blancos, rosas. Azules casi en veta,
    Retraídos, mentales.
Puntos de luz latente dan señales
    De una sombra secreta.

Pero el color, infiel a la penumbra,
    Se consolida en masa.
Yacente en el verano de la casa,
    Una forma se alumbra.

Claridad aguzada entre perfiles,
    De tan puros tranquilos,
Que cortan y aniquilan con sus filos
    Las confusiones viles.

Desnuda está la carne. Su evidencia
    Se resuelve en reposo.
Monotonía justa, prodigioso
    Colmo de la presencia.

Plenitud inmediata, sin ambiente,
    Del cuerpo femenino.
Ningún primor: ni voz ni flor. ¿Destino?
    ¡Oh absoluto Presente!

Nude

Whites, pinks. A pale blue swash,
  Withdrawn, imagined.
Points of light flash a hint
  Of secret shadow.

But color, unfaithful to the gloom,
  Consolidates.
Lying in the summer of the room
  A shape takes light.

And the sharp clarity of silhouettes—
  Out of purity, a hush—
Whose edges can abolish
  The confusion through which they cut.

The flesh is nude, its evidence
  Resolved at rest.
A just monotony, prodigious
  Hoard of presence.

The full sufficiency, immediate and complete,
  Of a woman's body. Not beauty,
Not voice nor bloom, however pleasant.
  Her destiny? Oh absolute present!

Este «Colmo de la presencia» posee un valor primordial aquí y en todo *Aire Nuestro*. También hay poemas con nostalgia del pasado. Pero la figura predominante no es la mujer ausente. (Lo es en la serie «In Memoriam», o como dice Petrarca, «in morte di Madonna Laura».) *Aire Nuestro* se inclina más bien a la exaltación de la presencia inmediata, modo menos frecuente en la historia de la poesía. Un ejemplo:

This "hoard of presence" is of utmost importance here and throughout *Aire Nuestro*. There are also poems that express nostalgia for the past. But the predominant figure is not the absent woman (as it is in the series "In Memoriam," or as Petrarch says, "in morte di Madonna Laura"). *Aire Nuestro* tends rather to exalt the immediate presence, a mode less frequent in the history of poetry. An example:

Invocación

Sabes callar. Me sonríe,
Amor, desnuda tu boca.

Una espera—como un alma
Que desenvuelve su forma—
Sobre los labios ondula,
Se determina, se aploma.
　　Yo quiero profundizar,
　　Profundizar—imperiosa,
　　Encarnizada ternura—
　　En tu frescor, en sus conchas.

Con el beso, bajo el beso
Te busco, te imploro toda,
Esencial, feliz, desnuda,
Radiante, consoladora.
　　Consuelo hasta el más recóndito
　　Desamparo de la sombra,
　　Consuelo por plenitud
　　Que a la eternidad afronta.

Sabes callar. Me sonríe,
Amor, desnuda tu boca.

Invocation

You know how to hush. Your naked mouth,
My love, smiles at me.

A hope—like a soul
Unfolding itself—
Hovers on your lips,
Takes shape, falls.
  I'd like to fathom,
  Fathom—commanding,
  Rosy-blushing tenderness—
  Your cool flesh, its conches.

With this kiss, beneath this kiss,
I seek you out, I entreat all of you,
You—essential, happy, naked,
Radiant, consoling.
  A consolation to the most far-flung
  Abandonment of darkness,
  The consolation of a plenitude
  That affronts eternity.

You know how to hush. Your naked mouth,
My love, smiles at me.

Es el segundo poema de una serie «La Isla». La isla amorosa se reduce aquí a una sucesión: el beso. Otra plenitud «Que a la eternidad afronta». ¿Eternidad? Es la perspectiva ilusoria que se repite . . . eternamente en el tiempo, y corresponde al deseo de algo que nunca se acaba. El poema se refiere al amor largo y logrado. Lo que no significa «perfecto». Eso sería idealismo falso, y no la realidad verdadera.

Vengamos a esa imperfección. En ese amor constante hay crisis—que no son definitivas y jamás conducirán a una ruptura. Lo resume cierto soneto: La parte central de *Cántico* se titula «El pájaro en la mano» y su sección central está compuesta de sonetos. Y el soneto central es «Mundo continuo»—con una cita de Shakespeare: banderita en esa cúspide de *Cántico*. (Pormenor que—dijo alguien en la intimidad—no lo verá ni Joaquín Casalduero, admirable crítico. Pero sí lo advirtió.) «And all in war with Time for love of you» (verso del soneto xv shakesperiano). El soneto no fue bien entendido. Un comentarista creyó que el poema se sitúa en la tradición de Jorge Manrique. Esta vez, la referencia a la tradición era equivocada. Último verso: «Su realidad va dando al mar el río». ¿A la muerte? No, todo lo contrario: a la vida, a su realización. (La segunda parte de *Clamor*, «. . . Que van a dar en la mar» alude exactamente a la significación manriqueña.) Entonces el autor—en vista de esa crítica equivocada—consultó con varios amigos críticos. Se comprobó así que a todos menos a uno, perturbaba la reminiscencia tradicional.

This is the second poem in the series "The Island." The island of love is here reduced to a single event: the kiss. Another fulfillment "that affronts eternity." Eternity? An illusory perspective that is repeated . . . eternally in time, and answers to a desire for something endless. The poem alludes to a long and fulfilled love. Which doesn't mean "perfect." That would be false idealism, not true reality.

Let's look at that imperfection. In this constant love there are crises—which are not definitive and will never lead to a break. It is summed up in a particular sonnet: The central part of *Cántico* is called "El pájaro en la mano" ("A Bird in the Hand") and its central section is composed of sonnets. And the central sonnet is "Continuous World"—with a quotation from Shakespeare: like a little flag on that peak of *Cántico*. (A detail which, as someone close to me said, not even that admirable critic, Joaquín Casalduero, will see. But in fact he did notice it.) "And all in war with Time for love of you" (Sonnet xv). My sonnet was misunderstood. One critic thought that the poem was in the tradition of Jorge Manrique.[3] On this occasion, the reference to tradition was mistaken. The last line: "The river spills itself into the sea." A movement toward death? No, quite the contrary, toward life, toward its fulfillment. (The second part of *Clamor*, ". . . Que van a dar en la mar" [". . . Which Lead to the Sea"] alludes precisely to that Manriquean meaning.) So the author, in view of that mistaken reading, consulted a number of critic friends. He found that this echo of the tradition bothered all but one.

Mundo continuo

And all in war with Time for love of you—SHAKESPEARE

Si amor es ya mi suma cotidiana,
Mundo continuo que jamás tolera
Veleidad de retorno a la primera
Nada anterior al Ser, que siempre gana,

Si cada aurora se desvive grana,
¿Por qué azares indómitos se altera
La fatalmente a salvo primavera,
Segura de imponer su luz mañana?

De pronto, bajo el pie, cruje un desierto
Con una flor de pétalos punzantes.
Aridez, lejanía, vil vacío.

Y mientras, por un rumbo siempre cierto,
Sin acción de retorno, como antes
Su realidad va dando al mar el río.

Continuous World

And all in war with Time for love of you—SHAKESPEARE

If love, now, is the sum of my every day,
A continuous world which will not tolerate
Velleities of return to that first Void
Before Being that does not know defeat;

If every dawn dies for the color scarlet—
Through what ungoverned accidents does spring,
Fatally safe and certain of its power
To impose its light on us tomorrow, change?

But now a desert crunches suddenly
Underfoot, sprouts its thorny flower.
Dryness and distance and bleak emptiness.

And meanwhile, by a straight and certain course,
Without a backward slip, just as before,
The river spills itself into the sea.

Había que registrar esos conflictos con el amor verdadero que sigue y sigue. Fijémonos en otro tipo de comunicación: «Carta urgente». (*Homenaje.*) Poema de ausencia. (Se cuida, a lo largo de la obra, de que no haya lagunas importantes.) Esta «Carta urgente» dirigida a la amada no se propone ser una epístola—en tercetos—acorde a este género clásico. Hay, sí, una forma moderna de la epístola en alejandrinos pareados según Ruben Darío, el fundamento de toda la poesía moderna en lengua española, como lo fue Baudelaire en Francia, en Europa.

It was important to write down those conflicts within a genuine love that goes on and on. Let's look at another kind of communication: "An Urgent Letter" (*Homenaje*). A poem about absence. (Throughout *Aire Nuestro* care has been taken not to leave any important gaps.) This "urgent letter" addressed to the loved one does not pretend to be an epistle—in tercets—in the tradition of that classical genre. There is, it's true, a modern form of the epistle in Alexandrine couplets invented by Rubén Darío,[4] the founder of all modern poetry in Spanish, as Baudelaire was in France and Europe in general.

Carta urgente

Te has ido. Me has dejado solo frente al deseo:
Mi afición a mezclarte con todo lo que veo,
A seguir tu perfume por esa escalerilla
Que nos lleva hasta el piso de una verdad sencilla:
Nada más necesario, más dulce ni más justo
Que unir en el coloquio tu gusto con mi gusto.
Y mi gusto va a ti, que ya te llamas «Tú»,
A quien digo: te quiero, je t'aime, I love you.
En cualquier lengua el verbo capital me conviene,
Y hasta muy bien callado también ti voglio bene.
Como aquí no te hallas, a este papel ahora
Le diré que eres tú quien tanto me enamora,
Y en esta soledad de diciembre quisiera
Dar a tu sola imagen valor de verdadera
Compañía. De modo muy leve me contento.
Vivimos en la forma precaria del momento.
Otra yo no conozco. ¿Soledades? Te has ido.
Ni tú ni yo sabemos de eclipse ni de olvido.
Ya no oteas quizá por el cristal del tren
El paisaje, tan tuyo. Y reclinas la sien
Para mejor soñar con los ojos cerrados.
Ah, tus ojos cerrados . . . Lo sé. No es que un abismo
Vaya a causarte vértigo. Nada existe a tus lados.
Quieres amar así. ¿Me ves? Soy tu amor mismo.

An Urgent Letter

You've gone. You've left me here with my desire:
My love of mixing you with all I see,
Of following your perfume along that stairway
That carries us up to a simple truth:
Nothing more sweet, more needed, nor more just,
Than to join both our wants in one colloquy.
And my pleasure seeks you out, whom I call *Tú*,
And I say *je t'aime*, *te quiero*, I love you.
In any tongue the verb of verbs will suit me
And even when I'm silent *ti voglio bene*.
Since you're not here, I take this page to say
That it is you who inspire me so, my love.
In this December solitude I'd like
To give your image all the value of
True company. In a light way I'm content.
We live in the risky confines of the moment.
I know no other way. And loneliness?
You've left me here. But neither you nor I
Know anything of oblivion or eclipse.
And looking out the window of the train
Perhaps you do not see that landscape now,
So much your own. You lean, you rest your head,
Eyes closed, the better to dream. Ah—you close
Your eyes. . . . I know. It's not that an abyss
Would give you vertigo. Nothing exists
At your side. That is how you want to love.
Do you see me? For love, it's me you miss.

«Soy tu amor mismo». Es un preludio de amor expresado en el tono y la manera de una carta . . . versificada. Amor, amistad, admiración constituyen los tres círculos concéntricos de toda la obra. Sobre la amistad se habla a través de *Aire Nuestro*. En la breve poesía «Los amigos» hay un verso que fue discutido: «Amigos. Nadie más. El resto es selva». «Ce vers réticent . . .», observa el crítico francés muy bueno Pierre Darmangeat. Esa «reticencia» se debe a la situación histórica en que fue escrito el poema. (Sevilla, guerra civil.) Si se tiene presente esa «circunstancia» se entenderá por qué se afirma: «El resto es selva». Selva feroz, que no se resuelve en caos. (Lo informe permanece, por supuesto, exterior a esta poesía.)

"It's me you miss." This is a prelude to love expressed in the tone and manner of a letter . . . in verse. Love, friendship, admiration constitute the three concentric circles of the whole work. Friendship runs throughout *Aire Nuestro*. In the short poem "Friends" there is a verse that provoked controversy: "Friends. No one else. The rest is wilderness." "Ce vers réti-cent," observed the fine French critic Pierre Darmangeat. That "reticence" is due to the historical circumstances in which the poem was written. (Seville, Civil War.) If you keep those "circumstances" in mind, you will understand why it says: "The rest is wilderness." A ferocious jungle, which does not dissolve into chaos. (The formless, of course, is left out of this poetry.)

Los amigos

Amigos. Nadie más. El resto es selva.
¡Humanos, libres, lentamente ociosos!
Un amor que no jura ni promete
Reunirá a unos hombres en el aire,
Con el aire salvándose. Palabras
Quieren, sólo palabras y una orilla:
Esos recodos verdes frente al verde
Sereno, claro, general del río.
¡Cómo resbalarán sobre las horas
La vacación, el alma, los tesoros!

Friends

Friends. No one else. The rest is wilderness.
But they—humane, free, idly indolent!
A love that neither promises nor swears
An oath will reunite some men
In the open air, to save themselves with air.
For words are what they want, words and a shore,
That's all: a tranquil bend
In the river's clear, pervading green.
How leisure, soul and riches
Will slip by, vagabonds across the hours!

«La vacación» ocurre junto al río aquí—o en otros muchos
y diversos lugares. Siempre será el tesoro del ocio.

We take our "leisure" here, next to the river—or in many other different places. It is always the reward of ease.

Tarde del 6 de diciembre de 1975

The Afternoon of December 6, 1975

Vamos a seguir ordenadamente este itinerario. Tras el amor y la amistad, el círculo tercero de la admiración. Admiración hacia la Naturaleza, las cosas, las relaciones del espíritu. Un poema de *Cántico*: «Amor a una mañana», en sentido metafórico, presenta una amistosa compenetración con una mañana de claridad.

Let's follow this itinerary in an orderly fashion. After love and friendship, the third circle: admiration. Admiration of nature, things, relations of the spirit. One poem in *Cántico*, "Love of a Morning" presents, in a metaphorical sense, a friendly communion with a bright clear morning.

Amor a una mañana

Mañana, mañana clara:
¡Si fuese yo quien te amara!

Paso a paso en tu ribera,
Yo seré quien más te quiera.

Hacia toda tu hermosura
Mi palabra se apresura.

Henos sobre nuestra senda.
Déjame que yo te entienda.

¡Hermosura delicada
Junto al filo de la nada!

Huele a mundo verdadero
La flor azul del romero.

¿De tal lejanía es dueña
La malva sobre la peña?

Vibra sin cesar el grillo.
A su paciencia me humillo.

¡Cuánto gozo a la flor deja
Preciosamente la abeja!

Y se zambulle, se obstina
La abeja. ¡Calor de mina!

El grillo ahora acelera
Su canto. ¿Más primavera?

Love of a Morning

Morning, clear morning!
If I could be your lover.

Along your shore, step by step,
I'll be the one who loves you more.

My word is drawn hastening
Toward all your loveliness.

Down our path we walk.
Let me understand the way you speak.

That such delicate beauty can hover
Next to the blade of the abyss!

The scent of the true world
Comes from the blue-petaled rosemary.

Is the mallow the mistress
Of such a stony retreat?

The cricket sings without stopping.
Such patience! I humble myself before him.

And the bee leaves such delight
To the blossom he bores in!

He dives in, he does not
Give up, despite the heat of mining for gold.

The cricket speeds up his song.
Can there be more of spring?

Se pierde quien se lo pierde.
¡Qué mío el campo tan verde!

Cielo insondable a la vista:
Amor es quien te conquista.

¿No merezco tal mañana?
Mi corazón se la gana.

Claridad, potencia suma:
Mi alma en ti se consuma.

Who loses this, is himself lost.
But this green field is surely meant for me!

Heavens whose great size
The eye cannot seize—you are conquered by love.

Do I not deserve such a morning?
Of itself, my heart wins this prize.

Clarity, highest power:
My soul will be perfected here.

Este pareado es lo que ordinariamente se denomina «aleluya». Forma popular empleada también en *Aire Nuestro*. De ahí, las varias reminiscencias. «La flor azul del romero» ya tradicional y en Góngora. «La malva sobre la peña» figura en una canción de la preciosa lírica galaico-portuguesa del XVI. «A su paciencia me humillo»; «humillo», recuerdo de Juan Ruiz para el autor. «Se pierde quien se lo pierde», con aire de copla andaluza. Todo ello, leído, vivido, se incorpora a ese verdadero fervor de alguien que goza directamente de esa frescura atmosférica en una mañana campesina. Y es el corazón quien «se la gana» mirando, respirando el paseante.

Podría coleccionarse un bestiario, un pequeño bestiario con los animales de *Aire Nuestro*. El hombre se adhiere en acto de admiración al vuelo de una gaviota, instante de pura vitalidad. (Sutton Island, Maine.)

This couplet is what is usually called an "aleluya," another popular form used in *Aire Nuestro*. Hence, various reminiscences. "The blue-petaled rosemary" is found in traditional poetry and in Góngora.[5] "Is the mallow the mistress / Of such a stony retreat?" appears in a song from that beautiful body of sixteenth century Galician-Portuguese lyric poetry. "I humble myself before him"; "I humble myself," an evocation for the author of Juan Ruiz.[6] "Who loses this, is himself lost," has the air of an Andalusian song. All this—read or lived—is incorporated into that true fervor of one who enjoys at first hand the freshness of a country morning. And it is the heart that "wins it," as the walker looks and breathes.

One could put together a bestiary, a little bestiary with all the animals in *Aire Nuestro*. In an act of admiration, man follows the flight of a sea-gull, a moment of pure vitality. (Sutton Island, Maine.)

Vuelo

Por el aire de estío
La gaviota ascendiendo
Domina la extensión, el mar, el mundo
Bajo azul, bajo nubes
En vellones muy blancos,
Y suprema, reinante,
Se cierne.

Todo el espacio es onda traspasada.

Plumajes blanquinegros
Detienen la ascensión,
De pronto resbalando sobre el aire,
Sobre la luz vastísima.

Sostiene la blancura del vacío.

Y, suspensas, las alas se abandonan
A claridad, a fondo trasparente
Por donde el vuelo, sin acción las alas,
Subsiste,
Se entrega a su placer, a su caer,
Se sume en su pasar,
Puro instante de vida.

Flight

Through summer air
The ascending gull
Dominates the expanse, the sea, the world
Under the blue, under clouds
Like the whitest wool-tufts,
And supreme, regal,
It soars.

All of space is a wave transfixed.

White and black feathers
Slow the ascent,
Suddenly slipping on the air,
On the vast light.

It buoys up the whiteness of the void.

And suspended, its wings abandon themselves
To clarity, to the transparent depths
Where flight, with stilled wings,
Subsists,
Gives itself entirely to its own delight, its falling,
And plunges into its own passing—
A pure instant of life.

Este último verso concentra la intención que ha movido a la pluma: hacer *sentir* un «instante de vida».

Continuemos con el mar, ahora en una noche portuguesa. La poesía cabe en una sola cláusula, y no por virtuosismo. El movimiento sintáctico va enlazando y trabando todos los elementos—del paisaje y de la cláusula—, y de este modo se logra una modulación.

The intention that moved the author's pen is concentrated in the last line: to make a "pure instant of life" felt.

Let us continue with the sea, now on a night in Portugal. The poem is contained in a single sentence, and not as a show of virtuosity. The syntactic movement weaves together, connects all the elements (of the landscape and of the sentence), and in this way achieves a modulation.

Mar con luna

Un cielo poco estrellado
Da a esta luna de sí llena
Fondo oscuro de contraste
Para el rayo que riela
Sobre un camino de mar
Medio acero, medio perla,
Grises blancos donde flotan
Barquichuelas, casi negras
Sobre la banda muy clara
De un agua que es luna extensa,
Luna derretida abajo
Frente a la que redondea
Su esbozo de faz viviente,
Nos preside, nos gobierna
Según hábitos serenos,
Y como hallándose cerca
Nos otorga una atención
De luz siempre dulce a fuerza
De gran familiaridad
Antigua con su planeta.

Sea with Moon

A nearly starless sky
Provides the full moon filled
With itself depths of darkness
In which the glistening ray
May ride on a sea-road,
Half-steel, half-pearl, grey-white
Ocean where tiny boats
Are bobbing, almost black
Against water that is
A clear band of bright moon
Pulled forth and melted down
Beneath the one that rounds
Itself out as a living
Face, and presides above,
And governs us according
To tranquil habits and
As if finding itself
Nearby, concedes to us
An attention of that light
Always sweet, out of great
Familiarity
With its planet of old.

En cierta poesía moderna sin ritmo o a contra-ritmo, las cosas están colocadas en el mismo plano. También en las imitaciones de Joyce en prosa de novela resalta más aún la falta de modulación. Modulación musical con sus altibajos armónicos; sucesiones que recorren diferentes niveles, contrapuestos a la inmovilidad de las cosas sobre una sola monotonía. Desde «Un cielo poco estrellado» se desciende por escala—verso a verso—hasta un «agua que es luna extensa». Y la modulación nos remonta—en sonido y en sentido—hasta la luna que «Nos preside, nos gobierna», más cercana por fin, en «familiaridad / Antigua con su planeta».

Mencionemos alguna poesía de admiración en acto de rigurosa admiración a obras y personajes, sobre todo poetas. Un ejemplo: Fray Luis de León. Puede suceder que la lectura de un clásico manifieste afinidades con los gustos del lector. Fray Luis es un gran poeta en dos direcciones: la afirmativa y la negativa. (Coincidencia con *Aire Nuestro*.) Fray Luis percibe la armonía de las esferas según Pitágoras, según Platón y, por otra parte, siente el drama humano, que ha sufrido con intensidad extraordinaria. Aquel fraile y profesor—los dos claustros, el del Convento y el de la Universidad—sin apenas salir de Salamanca, sin historias de amor ni de viaje ni de política ni dinero, vivió íntegramente el drama humano. Sus colegas en la universidad y en el convento fueron suficientes para que Fray Luis aprendiera lo que es la existencia del hombre. ¡Cinco años de Inquisición! He aquí la semblanza y el elogio.

In a certain kind of unrhythmical or anti-rhythmical modern poetry, everything in the poem is placed on the same level. In the imitations of Joyce in the novel this lack of modulation is even more apparent. A musical modulation with its harmonic contrasts; successions that move from level to level, counterposed to the immobility of things in a single monotone. From "A nearly starless sky" down the scale— line by line—to "water that is / A clear band of bright moon." And this modulation takes us back—in sound and sense—to the moon that "presides above, / And governs us," closer at last, "out of great / Familiarity / With its planet of old."

Let's turn to some poems of praise in an act of rigorous admiration for works and people, especially poets. An example: Fray Luis de León.[7] It can happen that the reading of a classic reveals affinities with the reader's taste. Fray Luis is a great poet in two directions: positive and negative. (Which coincides with *Aire Nuestro*.) Fray Luis perceives the harmony of the spheres (Pythagorean or Platonic), and yet he also feels the human drama, which he suffered with an extraordinary intensity. That friar and professor—in both cloisters, the Monastery and the University—scarcely leaving Salamanca, without any intrigues of love or travel or politics or money, lived the human drama in its entirety. His colleagues in the university and in the monastery sufficed for Fray Luis to learn what man's existence is. Five years of Inquisitorial persecution! Here is his portrait and his praise.

Fray Luis de León

El aire se serena,
Por claridad regala más espacio,
Maestro, cuando suena
La lira que a tu Horacio
No fue más fiel ni dio más gloria al Tracio.

Oías el acorde
Reservado a tu alma en el silencio
Total de las estrellas,
O compartías música en la pausa
Del ocio con amigos.

Todo es número, tácito o sonoro.
Entre sus concordancias te conducen
Pitágoras, Platón.
                Y arriba, Cristo,
Centro, ya no doliente.

El doliente eres tú, que estás abajo,
En tu brega diaria
Con el ceño severo del pedante,
Con el adusto hipócrita,
Por claustros de una envidia
Que a los colegas trueca en tu envolvente
Plaga devoradora.

¡Cuántos colegas bajo las esferas!

Jamás se abolirán aquellos números
Esenciales, que escuchas
Por entre los teólogos sutiles,

Fray Luis de León

The air sweetens,
Through clarity bestows more space,
Master, when that lyre
Sounds which to your Horace
Was not more true, nor gave more fame to Thrace.

You heard the concord
Reserved for your soul in the utter
Silence of the stars,
Or you shared music, in a peaceful
Moment with your friends.

All is number, silent or sounded.
Pythagoras and Plato guide you
Through their harmonies.
                              And above, Christ,
The Center, no longer suffering.

The suffering one is you, below,
In your daily fray
With the pedant's strict frown,
With the grim hypocrite,
Through cloisters of an envy
Which transforms your colleagues into
A surrounding, devouring plague.

So many colleagues beneath the spheres!

Those essential numbers, which you hear
Among the subtle theologians
Always struggling hand to hand

Siempre a brazo partido
Con el mal y sus máscaras.

¿Te hace sufrir el tonto,
Te ensombrece el opaco, tan robusto?
Toda la algarabía
Desemboca al silencio.

Silencio de que parte, llano liso,
La música—de cifras
Mentales, o de estrellas,
O del rabel sagrado.

Y no habrá confusión,
Aunque tan cruelmente
Desgarre tus entrañas,
Que no quede por fin inmersa en mundo,
El mundo enorme que lo abarca todo,
La inmundicia, la flor, el verso bueno,
Sin cesar turbamulta
De Creación en creación. ¡Oh vida,
Aquí mismo inmortal!

El aire se serena. Luz no usada.

With evil and its masks,
Will never be abolished.

Does the idiot torment you,
Does the dullard—so robust!—sadden you?
All the senseless jabber
Ends in silence.

A silence, smooth and plain, from which
The music springs—music of mental
Ciphers, or of the stars,
Or of the sacred rebeck.

And there will be no confusion,
Although it tears
Cruelly at your entrails,
That does not at last remain immersed in the world,
The great world that embraces all—
Filth, flowers, the good poem,
The ceaseless swirling rabble
Of Creation, in creation. Oh life
Everlasting even here!

The air sweetens. An unaccustomed light.

La primera estrofa es una lira, estilo Fray Luis: una devota imitación para empezar, «El aire se serena». Oda a Francisco Salinas. Música del cielo estrellado y música del rabel, instrumento de entonces. La música del amigo profesor de aquella Universidad es la compartida «en la pausa del ocio con amigos»: un concierto para un grupo de humanistas. Esta visión histórica se opone a la interpretación de la Oda al músico de Salamanca como un poema místico. «A este bien os llamo, amigos / a quien amo sobre todo tesoro, / que todo lo demás es triste lloro». Asistió a uno de aquellos conciertos el humanista Ambrosio de Morales, y le pareció que asistía a la Academia de Platón. Y allí también, entre los claustros, el conflicto: «¡Cuántos colegas bajo las esferas!» Lo que no impide que «El mundo enorme que lo abarca todo» sea, en definitiva, una «turbamulta / De Creación». Y volvemos *da capo*: «El aire se serena. Luz no usada».

Otro homenaje al último poeta genial anterior a la Guerra Civil. Miguel Hernández fue un hombre de campo, un alma buena, un pastor genial.

The first stanza is a "lira," in the style of Fray Luis: a devout imitation to begin, "The air sweetens." The Ode to Francisco Salinas. Music of the star-filled skies and music of the rebeck, an instrument of that time. The music of his friend (also a professor at the University of Salamanca), is shared "in a peaceful / Moment with your friends": a concert for a group of Humanists. This historical vision opposes the interpretation of Fray Luis' "Ode" as a mystical poem. "I call you, friends, to this pleasure / You, whom I love above all treasure, / For the rest is tearful sorrow." The humanist Ambrosio de Morales attended one of those concerts, and it seemed to him that he was in Plato's Academy. And there, too, in the cloisters, conflict: "So many colleagues beneath the spheres!" Which in no way impedes "the great world that embraces all" from being a "ceaseless swirling rabble / Of Creation." And we return, *da capo*: "The air sweetens. An unaccustomed light."

Another homage, this one to the last great poet before the Civil War. Miguel Hernández[8] was a country boy, a good soul, a shepherd genius.

Miguel Hernández

Era el don de sí mismo
Con arranque inocente,
La generosidad
Por exigencia y pulso
De aquel ser, criatura
De fuego—si no barro,
O ya vidrio con luz que lo traspasa.

Así, de claridades fervoroso,
Encuentra fatalmente su aliado
Más íntimo, más fiel
En ciertos cuerpos leves.
¡Palabras! Signos muy reveladores
Van alumbrando un más allá, descubren
Un mundo fresco, gracia.

Este aprendiz perpetuo de las formas,
Pretéritas, actuales, ya futuras,
Es al fin absorbido
Por un grave tumulto
Que lo arroja al extremo de su dádiva.
Mujer, el hijo, lucha. Lucha atroz,
Límite esperanzado.

Genial: amor, poema.
Español: cárcel, muerte.

Miguel Hernández

He was his own gift to himself,
With impetuous innocence,
Generous
Out of the necessity and pulse
Of his being—a child
Of fire, if not clay,
Or now glass shot through with light.

And so, zealous for clarity,
He finds his inevitable,
Most intimate, most faithful allies
In certain airy bodies.
Words! The revealing signs
Light up the unknown, discover
A new world, and grace.

This perpetual apprentice of forms
Past present and future
Is at last caught up
In a mortal turmoil
That throws him to the extreme of his powers.
Wife, child, struggle. Brutal struggle,
Hope to the end.

Brilliant: love, poem.
Spanish: prison, death.

El poema alude a su gran don expresivo, a la intensidad con que ahondó las palabras, «cuerpos leves», aquel «aprendiz . . . de las formas», que asimiló influencias del Siglo de Oro, Lope, Calderón. Después vino para aquella criatura de amor el «grave tumulto», la «lucha atroz», la cárcel, la muerte.

A veces la ironía se une a la admiración. Este humorismo existe ya en *Cántico*, y los volúmenes posteriores lo desarrollan más y más. Un recuerdo de una visita al Metropolitan Museum de Nueva York, una tarde, en verano, es:

This poem alludes to his great expressive gift, to the intensity with which he delved into words, "airy bodies," that "apprentice of forms," who assimilated influences of the Golden Age: Lope, Calderón. Then to that child of love came "mortal turmoil," "brutal struggle," jail, death.

At times irony is joined to admiration. A sense of humor was already present in *Cántico*, and is developed even more in the later volumes. The memory of a visit to the Metropolitan Museum of New York, one summer afternoon.

Mirar y admirar

Me detengo. Lo adiviné: Tiziano.
Un gran señor otea varias diosas.
También yo me complazco en los follajes
Y su cobrizo tono así lejano.
¿Quiénes aquellas damas sobre losas
De galerías y azoteas? Trajes
Oscuros, pero . . .
A mi lado, real, está una dama.
No me ve. Soy un cero
—Soy realidad—ante ella, que reclama
Pintura.
Mi vista se aventura
Con un fervor cortés
—En mí cortés costumbre—
Por la forma viviente,
Que jamás ni comparo ni confundo
Con el fingido mundo,
Ahora Veronés.
No hay Venus de verdad que no relumbre
Sin mi adhesión y mi vivir no aliente,
Ahora también, que mal o apenas veo
—Otro piso propone el gran museo—
Esta flor de Matisse. Atrae la dama.
¿Fugitiva? No importa. ¡Cómo llama!

Double Vision

I stop. I knew it: Titian.
A grandee spies
On several goddesses. I too
Am happy hidden in the leaves
And their coppery, distant hue.
Who are those ladies
On the flagstones of roofs and rooms?
Dark costumes, but. . . .
At my side, real enough, stands
A woman. She does not see me.
I am a zero—I am reality—
For her, because she demands
Art.
My glance will dare
To venture out, courteous and eager—
In me, a habit of courtesy—
To the living form,
Which I never confuse or compare
With the imitation world—
At the moment hailing from the Verona of old.
There's no true Venus who does not glow
Without my embrace, who does not put a zing
In my blood. Even now,
When I can scarcely see
(And the museum offers another wing!)
This flower by Matisse.
The woman enthralls.
Does she flee? No matter. How she calls!

Se mira y se admira, pues, el arte y una dama, «forma viviente», sin confundir lo uno con lo otro. Esta aplicación visual en sitio público se entiende mejor entre latinos, por supuesto, que entre anglosajones. A la orilla del Mediterráneo se desenvuelve como un ejercicio muy natural.

Llegamos en nuestra ordenación a la parte crítica. El contacto con la realidad, por de pronto físico, intuitivo con su arrastre de sentimiento, implica también inteligencia que juzga. Podría llamarse juicio vital. Algo se acepta o se rehusa más o menos, y frente a la realidad inmediata. ¿Una actitud moralizante? Más bien un sentimiento de la vida. Hay acuerdo o hay desacuerdo. Este instante crítico no es función posterior, sino del proceso mismo del vivir. Crítica que puede ser grave o leve. Hay drama, hay comedia también. El autor de *Aire Nuestro* es muy sensible, y cada día más, a la comedia humana en cuanto comedia. (Se dice a sí mismo en ciertos monólogos: Si yo tuviese una segunda existencia, sería autor cómico . . .)

Aquel tema—tan repetido desde *Cántico*—del amanecer y el despertar admite en esa primera serie el tratamiento irónico. En este gallo—burlesco—del amanecer, se caricaturiza la afirmación del Yo, hinchado por soberbia, siempre condenada.

You look at and admire, then, art and a woman, a "living form," never confusing one with the other. This visual assiduousness in a public place is better understood among Latins, of course, than among Anglo-Saxons. On the shores of the Mediterranean it is practiced as a very natural activity.

We reach that part of our anthology devoted to criticism. Contact with reality, immediately physical and intuitive with its emotional charge, implies also a critical intelligence. It could be called vital judgement. Something is accepted or rejected, to a greater or lesser degree, and always in the face of immediate reality. A moralizing attitude? Rather a feeling for life. One agrees or disagrees. This critical instant does not occur after the fact, but is part of the very process of living. Criticism that can be serious or slight. There is drama, but there is also comedy. The author of *Aire Nuestro* is more and more sensitive to the human comedy as comedy. (He says to himself in certain monologues: If I had another life, I would write comedies. . . .)

The theme of dawning and awakening—so frequently repeated from *Cántico* on—receives an ironic treatment in that first series. This ludicrous rooster crowing at dawn caricatures the affirmation of the "I," swollen with pride, eternally damned.

Gallo del amanecer

(Sombras aún. Poca escena.)
Arrogante irrumpe el gallo.
—Yo.
    Yo.
        Yo.
            ¡No, no me callo!

Y alumbrándose resuena,
Guirigay
De una súbita verbena:
—Sí.
    Sí.
        Sí.
            ¡Quiquiriquí!

—¡Ay!
Voz o color carmesí,
Álzate a más luz por mí,
Canta, brilla,
Arrincóname la pena.

Y ante la aurora amarilla
La cresta se yergue: ¡Sí!
(Hay cielo. Todo es escena.)

Chanticleer

(Shadows still. A scene half-lit.)
The proud cock cries out:
  "I!
    I!
      I!
        I'll not be silent!"

And again, drunk with daybreak,
The bright glee
Of a sudden flight:
  "Me!
        Me!
            Me!
                Quiquiriquí!"

Ay!
Plumes or voice of sheer crimson,
Fly up to the light for my sake,
Sing, shine!
Make all my pain be gone.

And before the wide yellow dawn
The cock's comb rises: Hie!
(Sky. The stage is set.)

A «la aurora amarilla» corresponde la «voz o color carmesí». Al sonido agudo y brillante de la vocal *i*—central, «sí», «quiquiriquí»—se le siente amarillo o rojo. En suma: «La cresta se yergue: ¡Sí!» En clave irónica, el núcleo de *Aire Nuestro*.

Tras un gallo, un demonio. «Luzbel desconcertado» es el poema más cuantioso de toda la obra, quinientos versos: un monólogo de Luzbel, el diablo capital en persona, con diversos tonos y escenas. Se ha escogido para la lectura una escena cómica: el homenaje a un gran poeta en su patria. No se refiere esta figura a ningún artista contemporáneo. Algún lector malicioso pensó en . . . ¡No, de ninguna manera! A Juan Ramón Jiménez le gustaba mucho el elogio. Recordemos lo que en el *Viaje del Parnaso* se atreve a decir Cervantes de Góngora: «Don Luis de Góngora, / a quien temo ofender con mis grandes alabanzas, / aunque las lleve al grado más supremo». Al gran poeta cordobés le ofendían siempre los elogios, insuficientes. (Un caso análogo: a Ortega, tan admirado por el autor de *Aire Nuestro*, se le podía atacar, pero elogiar . . . ¡No, por Dios!) En este pasaje de Luzbel se censura una vez más la soberbia, el gran pecado del espíritu.

The "plumes or voice of sheer crimson" correspond to the "wide yellow dawn." The sharp and brilliant sound of the vowel "i"—central to the poem: "sí," "quiquiriquí"—is felt as yellow or red. In short: "The cock's comb rises: Hie!" In an ironic key, the nucleus of *Aire Nuestro*.

First a rooster, then a devil. "Lucifer Confounded" is the longest poem of the entire work, five hundred lines: a monologue delivered by Lucifer, the head devil in person, diverse in tone and scene. A comic scene has been chosen for this reading: an homage to a great poet in his own country. This figure does not reflect any contemporary artist. A malicious reader thought of. . . . No! By no means! Juan Ramón Jiménez[9] loved praise. Remember what Cervantes dares to say of Góngora in the *Viaje del Parnaso*: "Don Luis de Góngora, / whom I fear to offend with my great praises, / though I carry them to the highest degree." The great poet from Córdoba was always offended by praise, because it was always insufficient. (A similar case: Ortega y Gasset,[10] greatly admired by the author of *Aire Nuestro*, could be attacked, but praised . . . God forbid!) In this passage from "Lucifer . . ." pride, the great sin of the spirit, is censured once again.

de Luzbel desconcertado

Gobernador: Vedle pálido,
Mareado ante el deliquio
Con que le acoge su pueblo.
Poeta: (¡Ay! Si no enmudeces, chillo.
Me quiere ofender, me insulta.
¡A «mi pueblo» reducido,
Por entre las dimensiones
De su tamaño ridículo!)
G.: Después de tal ovación,
El Maestro va a deciros
Unas palabras.
P.: ¡Auxilio!
Yo no sé lo que me pasa.
(Mi paciencia no ha podido
Resistir el homenaje.)
Estoy enfermo.
G.: ¡Divino
Paisano!
P.: ¡Por Dios! De veras
Estoy mal. Yo no soy divo.
No puedo hablar. No hablaré.
(¡Insolentes! Lo han urdido
Todo contra mí. ¡Primero
De mi país, qué ludibrio,
De mi tiempo nada más!)

from Lucifer Confounded

Governor: See him pale,
Unnerved by the rapture with which
His people welcome him.
Poet: (Ay! If you will not be
Silent, I'll scream. He wants
To offend me, he insults me.
Reduced to "my people,"
Belittled to their own
Ridiculous dimensions!)
G.: After such an ovation,
The Maestro will pronounce
A few words for us.
P.:   Help!
I cannot understand
What's happening to me.
I cannot even endure
This homage. And I'm ill.
G.: Our divine countryman!
P.: My God! I'm really not
Feeling very well.
I'm no prima donna.
I cannot speak. I will
Not speak. (Such insolence!
They have schemed against me.
The foremost of my country—
What a mockery!
Merely first of my time!)

G.: Señores, no somos dignos
De escuchar al gran poeta.
Aplaudidle: es el cautivo
Doliente de este fervor.
¡Miradle! ¡Visto y no visto!

G.: Gentlemen, we ourselves
     Are not worthy to hear
     The great poet. Applaud
     Him, yes, the suffering
     Captive of this fervor.
     But look at him now:
     Visible and invisible!

A esto se llega por la vía de la sátira, lo que se llamaba sátira en la antigüedad grecolatina. Esta escena es el extremo satírico hasta donde se alarga *Aire Nuestro*.

Otro texto, breve: «Para no engreírse». Sátira en que se alude a Cristo—al César lo que es del César—, y saltando sobre abismos, a personajes históricos: el siniestro Eichmann, que murió en Israel, y el marqués de Sade. La sátira comporta, claro, un fondo moral. Y por fin, surge un gato, quieto al sol muy dignamente.

This effect is achieved through satire—what was called satire in Classical Antiquity. This scene represents the satirical extreme reached in *Aire Nuestro*.

Another text, this one short: "So As Not To Become Too Vain." A satire alluding to Christ—render therefore unto Caesar the things which are Caesar's—and, leaping a great chasm, to historical personages: the sinister Eichmann, who died in Israel, and the Marquis de Sade. Satire, of course, carries an implicit moral intention. At the end, a cat appears, lying calmly, nobly in the sun.

Para no engreírse

Al ser superior acato.

«Dad
Al César lo que es del César»,
Y al gato lo que es del gato.

¡Gato!

Jamás un Eichmann o un Sade
Con
Crímenes de razón.

Bajo un sol de silencio
                        tan digno en soledad.

So As Not To Become Too Vain

I venerate the superior being.

"Render therefore
Unto Caesar the things which are Caesar's,"
And unto the cat, those things which are the cat's.

The cat!

Never an Eichmann or a Sade
With their
Crimes of reason.

Under a silent sun,
                    so august in solitude.

¿Cuántas veces hemos pensado todos que ha habido en nuestra época monstruos infinitamente inferiores a muchos animales? Todos estos poemas conciernen al «Tiempo de Historia». Historia sobre todo contemporánea. También de *Clamor* en adelante se incluyen diversas personalidades históricas. A la experiencia personal se añade la experiencia de la cultura, de mayor radio.

Se parte, como premisa ineludible, de cierta cultura, vivida tanto como cualquier otra actividad, y de modo auténtico. (No puede quedar más lejos el pedante.) El vino en el borracho no es más vital que el libro que se lee o estudia sin embriaguez. Esta consideración de la Historia puede ser afirmativa o negativa. ¿Son numerosos los horrores? Pero también el hombre ha hecho cosas admirables. Comencemos por la admiración. El autor de *Aire Nuestro* pasó por Rotterdam, y se quedó asombrado. La ciudad destruida por los bombardeos nazis en Holanda, ha sido totalmente rehecha. Cualquier viajero tiene que sentirse atónito.

How many times have we all thought that there have been monsters in our time, much worse than many animals? All these poems concern the "Time of History"—above all, contemporary history. And from *Clamor* on, many different historical persons are included. To personal experience is added the broader area of cultural experience.

A certain level of culture, lived as genuinely as any other activity, is an unavoidable premise of this poetry. (Which is anything but pedantry. Wine is no more vital to the drunkard than books to the clear-headed reader.) This consideration of history can be positive or negative. If there are innumerable atrocities, nonetheless man has done admirable things, as well. Let's begin with admiration. The author of *Aire Nuestro* travelled through Rotterdam, and was amazed. This Dutch city, completely destroyed by Nazi bombing, has been totally rebuilt. This cannot fail to astonish any traveler.

Historia extraordinaria

. . . Y bajo los diluvios demoníacos,
Reiterada la furia
Con método,
Fue conseguida—casi—
La destrucción total.
Y cayeron minutos, meses, años.
Y no creció entre ruinas
El amarillo jaramago solo,
Amarillo de tiempo,
De un tiempo hueco a solas.
Se elevaron los días, las semanas.
Y vertical, novel,
Surgió el nombre de siempre.
Ya Rotterdam es Rotterdam.
¡Salud!

Creo en la voluntad
De este planeta humano:
Planeta de alimañas,
De velludos feroces que en dos pies
Se alumbran con los fuegos que sus artes
Encienden,
Fuegos, ay, tan ambiguos,
De anulación y de invención, hermanas,
Las hermanas gemelas
Sumisas o insumisas
A este bronco animal
Que, ceñido de bosques,
Va de idea en idea trasformando
La realidad, a veces
Del todo realizada.

History of a Marvel

. . . And under the satanic deluge,
The fury methodically
Reiterated,
The result was
An almost total destruction.
And the minutes, the months, the years, fell.
And among the ruins
The yellow mustard did not grow alone,
Yellow with time,
An empty solitary time.
The days, the weeks rose higher,
And towering, new,
The old name ascended.
Again Rotterdam is Rotterdam.
Salud!

I believe in the will
Of this human planet:
Planet of predators,
Of shaggy brutes up on two feet
Who light their drunken hours with fires their arts
Have kindled,
Ambiguous fires—
Twin sisters of destruction and creation,
Submitting to this coarse animal
Or rebelling, while he,
Surrounded by forests,
Hops from idea to idea transforming
What is real—and at times
Fashioning it perfectly.

Gloria a la bestia convertida en hombre.
Entre apuros y angustias
Candidato a lo humano,
Asciende hasta la cumbre de su espíritu:
Nada más una chispa.
Y luce,
Alegre, más, terrible. ¡Qué de hogueras,
Qué de chisporroteos, surtidores
Nocturnos, faustos brillos!
Las olas y las tierras y las brisas,
Nombradas, se someten,
Y hasta el áspero prójimo dibuja
Su perfil dominante
De montañas, de ríos, de confines.
«Hacer» tendrá más radio que «soñar».

En este muelle, frente a embarcaciones
Y grúas y horizontes,
Siento inmortal a Europa,
Uno siento el planeta.
La historia es sólo voluntad del hombre.

Glory to the beast changed to man.
A candidate for manhood
In his trials and testings,
He ascends to the peak of his spirit:
A mere spark.
And he shines.
He is happy and he is terrible. What bonfires,
What fiery sputterings, nocturnal
Jets, gaudy splendors!
Waves and earth and wind,
Once named, now submit,
And even the gruff neighbor turns to trace
His own dominating shape
On mountains, rivers, borders.
"To do" will reach farther than "To dream."

On this pier, before ships,
Cranes, horizons,
I feel that Europe is immortal,
That the planet is one.
History is simply the will of man.

Valga como conclusión: «La historia es siempre voluntad del hombre». Esto es, al menos, lo que este poeta cree.

¿Y el drama social? Dramas atroces. La sátira de la sociedad, sobre todo contemporánea, conlleva generales reflejos de la época; pero atiende con particular interés a España, a la Guerra Civil y sus consecuencias. Hay textos largos, desde «Potencia de Pérez» y «La sangre al río» hasta «Guirnalda Civil» y «Arte rupestre». Citaremos una poesía corta. Es un recuerdo del año 36: una prisión, no «prisiones» como dice Silvio Pellico.

Let this be our conclusion: "History is always the will of man." This, at least, is what the poet believes.

And social drama? Atrocious scenes. In *Aire Nuestro*, social satire, especially of contemporary society, reflects the historical period in general; but it pays particular attention to Spain, to the Civil War and its consequences. There are long texts, from "The Powers of Pérez" and "La sangre al río" ("Blood in the River") to "Guirnalda civil" ("Civil Garland") and "A Rupestrian Art." We will read a short poem. It is a memory of 1936: a prison, not "prisons" as Silvio Pellico[11] says.

Una prisión

(1936)

Aquel hombre no tuvo nunca historia,
Pero tenía Historia como todos
Los hombres. Cierta crisis . . . Le apenaba
Recordar. Una vez habló, sereno.

Evoco mi prisión, no «mis prisiones».
Fue muy breve mi paso por la cárcel.
Cárcel en horas de mortal peligro.
Nos rodeaban sólo fratricidas.

«¿Hoy la suerte común será mi suerte:
Que sin forma de ley se me fusile
En nombre del Eterno, aquí tan bélico,

De sus milicias y de sus devotos?»
Confiar en mi estrella fue mi ayuda.
—¿No en Dios?—Andaba con los asesinos,

Según los asesinos y sus cómplices.

A Prison

(1936)

That man had no history of his own;
Like every other man, though, History
He did have. And it pained him to recall. . .
A certain crisis. Once, serene, he spoke.

I conjure up my prison, not "my prisons."
The time I spent in jail was very brief.
Jail—in those hours of mortal peril we were
Surrounded by a horde of fratricides.

"Today will my fate be the common one?
Without process of law, will I be shot
In the name of the Eternal—here so warlike—

And of its own soldiers, its votaries?"
My only recourse was to trust my star.
—And not God?—No, He walked beside assassins,

According to the assassins and their cohorts.

El prisionero tenía entonces confianza en su estrella. ¡Confianza absurda! —¿Y Dios?—le preguntó, mucho más tarde, una amiga. La respuesta se halla en los últimos versos. Los asesinos, sí, «los asesinos» alardeaban de contar con Dios.

No dejaremos a un lado «Potencia de Pérez». Pérez es sin duda nombre respetable, y a la vez, el nombre vulgar por antonomasia. (Una fuente cómica: «El terrible Pérez», sainete de Arniches sobre un Don Juan pequeño burgués. Refiriéndose a ciertos dictadores de nuestro tiempo salió en la conversación con Pedro Salinas aquel título. «Son tan mediocres, tan vulgares, los terribles Pérez». Comentó Salinas: «Lástima que eso no se pueda traducir».)

At that time, the prisoner trusted in his star. An absurd trust! And what about God, a friend asked him many years later. The answer is to be found in the final lines of the poem. The assassins, yes, "the assassins" were proud to count God among their number.

We cannot leave aside "The Powers of Pérez." Pérez is doubtless a perfectly respectable name, and at the same time, it is a very common Spanish name. (A literary source: "The Terrible Pérez," a comic skit by Arniches[12] about a petty bourgeois Don Juan. Referring to certain dictators of our time, this title came up in a conversation with Pedro Salinas.[13] "The terrible Pérezes are so mediocre, so vulgar," said Salinas, and he added: "It's a shame that can't be translated.")

Potencia de Pérez

Hay ya tantos cadáveres
Sepultos o insepultos,
Casi vivientes en concentraciones
Mortales,
Hay tanto encarcelado y humillado
Bajo amontonamientos de injusticia,
Hay tanta patria reformada en tumba
Que puede proclamarse
La paz.
Culminó la Cruzada. ¡Viva el Jefe!

El Jefe, solo al fin,
Cierra la puerta, siente alivio.
                                        Solo,
Sin el peso de un mundo abominable,
Sin la canalla que le adora y teme,
Que le adora y detesta.
Es él quien todos alzan para todos,
Y en ellos estribado,
Se aúpa,
Adalid de su Dios.
La victoria es santísima.

¡Sí! Se columbra junto al Jefe a Dios,
Tan propicio a la causa.
Una común empresa los reúne.

¿Cómo entender que un hombre, sólo un hombre
Doblegue a tantos bárbaros unidos
En vientos
De acosos homicidas,

The Powers of Pérez

There are now so many bodies
Buried or unburied,
Not quite alive in mortal
Concentrations,
There are so many jailed and humiliated,
Under great heaps of injustice,
So much of the nation lies reformed in the tomb
That peace
Can be proclaimed.
The Crusade is over. Long live the Chief!

The Chief, alone at last,
Closes the doors, welcomes his ease.
                                    Alone,
Without the weight of an abominable world,
Without the mob that fears and adores him,
Adores and detests him.
They have elevated him in their own behalf
And on their backs
He rises,
God's own chieftain.
Victory is most holy.

Yes! Next to the Chief, they spy God,
Who was so favorable to the cause.
A common enterprise unites them.

How could a man, one single man,
Drive so many thronged barbarians
Into winds
Of homicidal pursuit?

O en grupos de cabezas más agudas
Que ese cerebro acorde a tal fajín?

Fajín hay de Cruzado fulgurante,
Ungido por la Gracia
Del Señor, que es el guía.

Guía a través de guerra
Tan cruelmente justa
Para lanzar un pueblo a su destino.

Destino tan insigne
Que excluye a muchedumbres de adversarios
Presos o bajo tierra:
No votan, no perturban. ¡Patria unánime!

Sobreviven los puros,
De tan puros cubiertos
En el gran sacrificio
Por las sangres malvadas.

Oh Jefe, nunca solo: Dios te encubre.

Or into circles of minds quicker
Than the brain that won the General's sash?

The sash of a shining Crusader,
Anointed by the Grace
Of God, who is the guide.

Guide through a war
So cruelly perfect
For sending a people to their destiny.

Destiny so notable
It entirely denies the multitudinous adversary
Imprisoned or under the sod:
They do not vote, do not trouble anyone.
Unanimous nation!

The pure survive,
So pure in the great sacrifice
That they are covered with fiendish blood.

Oh Chief!—never alone: God will hide you.

«Culminó la Cruzada». En documentos oficiales se declaró que la Guerra Civil era una Cruzada religiosa. Todo aquel ambiente, en este aspecto, ha cambiado mucho. Citemos también un trozo de «Arte rupestre».

"The Crusade is over." In official documents the Civil War was declared a religious Crusade. That whole atmosphere, in this regard, has changed a great deal. Let's also read one section from "A Rupestrian Art."

de Arte rupestre

Durante siglos hubo un gran Imperio.
No podía durar eternamente
Ni sepulto yacer en cementerio.
Y alumbró el sol a un libre Continente.

(Se perdía batalla tras batalla.
El honor del guerrero en la derrota
Resplandecía sobre tanta falla
De su país con sueño de marmota.)

¡Cuántas Indias dejaron de ser presa
De aquel poder! Quedó profunda herida.
La metrópoli al fin, gloriosa empresa,
Fue la postrer colonia. ¡Sometida!

from A Rupestrian Art

For centuries imperial power stood firm.
But permanence for itself it could not win,
Nor lie entombed inside a churchyard wall.
While a continent was set free by the sun.

(All the battles, one by one, were lost.
The beaten warrior's honor was a gleam
Shining above the monstrous fault
Of his country, in a marmot's dream.)

So many Indies ceased to be the soils
Of Empire! Deep wounds, though, remained.
The mother-country, that glorious campaign,
Was itself the last conquest—the final spoils!

Durante siglos «hubo un gran imperio. . . ». Entonces, frente a un siglo tan nefasto en tantas direcciones, ¿no hay nada que hacer? Siempre se puede hacer algo en sentido positivo. Y tienen razón los americanos que así piensan. Sería inmoral, peor aún, sería mortal perder la esperanza. El final de «En estos años de tormentas», de alcance muy general, está formado por esta breve serie de versos.

For centuries "imperial power stood firm. . . ." Is there nothing to be done, then, in the face of a century so evil in so many ways? Something can always be done in a positive sense. And Americans are right to think this way. It would be immoral, worse even, it would be fatal, to lose hope. The end of "In These Tormented Years," is very general in meaning and consists of these few lines.

de En estos años de tormentas

Por entre los resquicios
Del Orden en desorden
Penetra una marea de conciencia,
Conato al fin de un coro.
El juego establecido continúa.
Allí está frente al juego
La presencia del coro
Con pulso ya de historia que gravita,
Que tiende hacia inserción
Real, hacia engranaje necesario.

from In These Tormented Years

Through the breach
In Order, a disorderly
Tide of conscience pours,
The effort at last of a chorus.
The established game continues.
There before it
Is the presence of that chorus
With the pulse now of history's lowering heft,
Tending toward the real
Insertion, toward the necessary meshing of the gears.

¡Ojalá!

Citemos también—de «En estos años de tormentas»—una poesía, «En la televisión», representativa de neustro Occidente en toda su amplitud.

Let us hope so!

Let's also read another poem from that group, "On Television," representative of our Western culture in its broadest sense.

En la televisión

Televisión. De pronto campo
Confuso de gentes, un día
Cualquiera.
       Si es guerra, no hay crimen.
Se ve a un prisionero. Camina
Con paso forzado hacia donde
Se concentra alguna milicia
Que sin más,
       vivir cotidiano,
—No hay pompa—dispara, fusila.
La figura del prisionero
Se doblega, casi caída.
Inmediatamente un anuncio
Sigue.
     Mercenarias sonrisas
Invaden a través de música.
¿Y el horror, ante nuestra vista,
De la muerte?
       Nivel a cero
Todo. Todo se trivializa.
Un caos, y no de natura,
Va sumergiendo nuestras vidas.
¿De qué poderío nosotros,
Inocentes, somos las víctimas?

On Television

Television. Suddenly a milling
Field of people, no day in
Particular.
                    If this is war, there is no crime.
A prisoner appears. He is marched
Toward where
Some soldiers cluster—
And they, without ado,
                              daily life,
—No ceremony—fire, execute.
The figure of the prisoner
Slumps, almost fallen.
Immediately there comes
A commercial.
                    Mercenary smiles
Invade with music.
And the horror, in our very sight,
Of death?
                    Everything at zero
Level, everything trivialized.
A chaos, and not nature's,
Comes over our lives submerging them.
What power holds us,
The innocent, as victims?

Este caso no es frecuente. En dos ocasiones hemos visto matar a un hombre en la televisión: tras el asesinato de Kennedy, el de su asesino, Oswald, y en la guerra del Vietnam, la ejecución de un «prisionero», que «se doblega. . . ». Y más horrendo, seguido por un inmediato anuncio. Este género de literatura no implica novedad, como creían algunos. Ya se ha dicho que la sátira siempre se ha cultivado, sobre todo desde Horacio, y en la literatura española, desde el «Libro de miseria de omne», «El Libro de Buen Amor», las «Coplas de Mingo Revulgo», etcétera. Un larguísimo etcétera. En la cumbre más alta, Dante, se encuentran enlazados los más diversos rumbos: religioso, ético, satírico, lírico, amoroso. Otros poetas, a muy desiguales niveles de valor, han intentado eso: una pequeña suma, no con más énfasis «summa».

This doesn't happen often. We have seen men killed on television on two occasions: in the wake of Kennedy's assassination, the murder of his assassin, Oswald; and during the Vietnam War, the execution of a "prisoner," who "slumps." And even more horrible, followed immediately by an advertisement.

This genre is not new to literature, as some have believed. As mentioned earlier satire has long been written, particularly since the time of Horace, and in Spanish literature, from the "Libro de miseria de omne," "El libro de buen amor," the "Coplas de Mingo Revulgo,"[14] etcetera. A very long etcetera. In Dante, the highest peak, all the different paths meet: the religious, the ethical, the satirical, the lyric, the amorous. Other poets, with very uneven results, have also tried this: a small sum, not a more emphatic "summa."

Mañana del 7 de diciembre de 1975

Morning of December 7, 1975

Llegamos al tema del tiempo. ¿Existe alguna poesía intemporal? «Intemporal» es abstracción, que no encaja en realidades. Las dos condiciones, espacio y tiempo, son requisitos ineludibles de la vida humana. Un viviente sin espacio sería tan incomprensible como un viviente sin tiempo. *Clamor*, segunda serie de *Aire Nuestro*, lleva como subtítulo *Tiempo de Historia*. Tiempo con fechas, historia colectiva y pública. Hay también un tiempo sin fechas, privado, íntimo. La parte central de *Clamor*, «. . . Que van a dar en la mar» se encuentra en ese tiempo, también histórico, pero sin cronología fechada: el recuerdo, la nostalgia del pasado, la conciencia de cómo va el hombre acercándose a la muerte, a través de las edades. En *Cántico* no hay viejos. Sólo infancia, juventud y madurez. Desde *Clamor* se van señalando las etapas de la ancianidad: se cumplen sesenta años, setenta años, ochenta años. Un soneto de *Cántico* se titula «Muerte a lo lejos». Después se tiene más conciencia de «cómo se viene la muerte / tan callando». Pero jamás se confunde la vida con la muerte. Por de pronto, la vida constituye un valor en la tierra. Y sin cesar el tiempo. Leamos un soneto de «. . . Que van a dar en la mar».

We arrive at the theme of time. Is there such a thing as timeless poetry? "Timeless" is an abstraction which does not fit the realities. Two conditions—space and time—are the unavoidable requisites of human life. An existence without space would be as incomprehensible as an existence without time. *Clamor*, the second series of *Aire Nuestro*, is subtitled *Time of History*. Time with dates, collective history, public history. There is also a private time, without dates, intimate. The central part of *Clamor*, ". . . That Lead to the Sea," is situated in that time—historical as well—but without a dated chronology: memory, nostalgia for the past, the awareness of man's passage, through the ages, toward death. In *Cántico* there are no old people. Just childhood, youth, maturity. After *Clamor* the different stages of old-age are marked: the sixtieth birthday, the seventieth, the eightieth. There is a sonnet in *Cántico* called "Death at a Distance." Later, there is a greater awareness of "how death approaches / so silently."[15] But life is never to be confused with death. For the moment, life is a value on earth. And time without end. Let's read a sonnet from ". . . That Lead to the Sea."

Del trascurso

Miro hacia atrás, hacia los años, lejos,
Y se me ahonda tanta perspectiva
Que del confín apenas sigue viva
La vaga imagen sobre mis espejos.

Aun vuelan, sin embargo, los vencejos
En torno de unas torres, y allá arriba
Persiste mi niñez contemplativa.
Ya son buen vino mis viñedos viejos.

Fortuna adversa o próspera no auguro.
Por ahora me ahinco en mi presente,
Y aunque sé lo que sé, mi afán no taso.

Ante los ojos, mientras, el futuro
Se me adelgaza delicadamente,
Más difícil, más frágil, más escaso.

Passage

I look back toward the distant years
So far, the long perspective gives
The cloudy image in the mirror
Such a narrow frame, it scarcely lives.

And yet, around the towers, the swifts
Still soar and dive, and there, on high,
My pensive early years persist.
My old vineyards give me good wine today.

Of fortune, good or bad, I have no hint.
For now, I grasp the present; though I know
What I know, I do not stint my verve.

The future, meanwhile, I observe
Diminishing for me, with delicate grace,
More difficult, more fragile, and more scant.

«En torno de unas torres». Torres de Valladolid. En el crepúsculo volaban los vencejos, contemplados por un niño. Aunque «el futuro» se adelgaza, más escaso, habrá siempre lucha mientras haya vitalidad. Al cumplirse ya setenta años se escribió este soneto «Al margen de Fernández de Andrade», el autor de la admirable «Epístola a Fabio».

"Around the towers"—towers of Valladolid. The swifts flew in the evening light, watched by a child. Although "the future" grows smaller, more scarce, there will always be a struggle as long as there is vitality. This next sonnet was written at the age of seventy: "In the Margin of Fernández de Andrade," author of the admirable "Epístola a Fabio."[16]

Cifras con cierto enfoque

¿Qué más que el heno a la mañana verde,
Seco a la tarde?

Los años, estos años que yo arrastro,
Pasan del seis al siete: ya setenta.
¿Soy yo esas cifras? ¿Son impedimenta
De fuera? ¿Son destino bajo un astro?

Poco a poco anochece en este claustro
Donde el silencio poco a poco aumenta,
Y entre las sombras late cenicienta
Luz que me trasparenta un alabastro.

El crepúsculo es noble si es sereno.
Mi reflexión me ayuda en este trance
De sentir que se pierde la partida.

A la memoria vuelve lo del heno
Seco al final. Difícil que no avance
Conmigo una penumbra desvalida.

Sums with a Particular Focus

¿Qué más que el heno a la mañana verde,
Seco a la tarde?

The years, these years that I drag after me
Change from six to seven: seventy now.
Am I these sums, are they the impedimenta
That I must haul? Some destiny of the stars?

Bit by bit it darkens in this cloister
Where silence bit by bit increases;
An ashen light is throbbing in the dimness
And glowing through transparent alabaster.

Twilight is noble when it is serene.
Reflection aids me, at this perilous point,
When I can sense that all the stakes are lost.

Memory restores the thought of that green hay,
Dry at day's end. Inevitable shadow
Must helplessly advance now at my side.

Sí, aumenta esa penumbra. Y los poemas van recogiendo ese sentimiento de vejez, lenta vejez gradual. Y en el horizonte, la muerte ya no lejana. El animal y el niño ignoran que son mortales. El presente y la presencia, sí, pero asimismo se profundiza esta *noción* de mortalidad, que no es ya acto de muerte, como nos repiten los estoicos, y algunos cristianos: Quevedo. El actual parlante, digan lo que digan, no va muriéndose ahora. ¿Vivir agónico en general? Un sofisma—«venerable sofisma» inadmisible. No hay ni un átomo de muerte en este normal momento de salud. Eso ocurrirá el último día. Ya en *Cántico* se afirma: una sola vez.

Indeed, the shadow deepens. And the poems increasingly reflect that feeling of old age, a slow and gradual aging. And on the horizon, death is no longer distant. Animals and children do not know that they are mortal. The present moment and presence, yes, but at the same time the *notion* of mortality becomes more profound; mortality which is not the act of death, as the Stoics, and some Christians—Quevedo[17]—would have it. The speaker of these words, say what they will, is not dying at this moment. Is life, then, a dying by degrees? A sophism—an inadmissible "venerable sophism." In this normal, hearty moment there is not even a particle of death. That will happen on the last day. This is already affirmed in *Cántico*: once only.

Una sola vez

Muerte: para ti no vivo.

¿Mientras, aguardando ya,
Habré de ahogarme en congojas
Diminutas soplo a soplo?

Espera.
　　　¡Sólo una vez,
De una vez!
　　　　　Espera tú.

¿Ves cómo el hombre persigue,
Por el aire del verano,
Más verano de otro ardor?

Vivo: busco ese tesoro.

Once Only

Death—it's not for you that I live.

Must I, expecting you already,
Choke on little
Anxieties breath by breath?

Wait.
    Only once,
And all at once!
          Wait, you.

See how a man will pursue,
Through the summer air,
More of summer, another ardor?

I am alive: I seek that treasure.

Contra esta breve poesía se escribió en polémica versificada. *Y Otros Poemas* contiene «El venerable sofisma».

> «Cada hora es la postrera.»
> Lo saben Dios y el Demonio.
> Confundid mortalidad
> Y muerte. ¡Sagrado embrollo!

Concluyamos con toda sencillez y del modo más elemental: la vida es vida y la muerte es muerte. Eso se dice en *Y Otros Poemas*:

This short poem sparked a polemic in verse. *And Other Poems* includes "The Venerable Sophism":

> "Every hour is the last,"
> As God and the Devil know.
> Confuse mortality, if you must,
> With death. Holy imbroglio!

Let us conclude in the simplest and most elementary way possible: life is life and death is death. From the volume *And Other Poems*:

Este muerto

I

Psique. La mariposa
Más tenue, trasparente.
Menos: la trasparencia
Del aire, sin sustancia
Visible. Quizá aroma
De flor perecedora.
¿Soy fragancia inmortal?

II

La vida es vida. Ay, la muerte es muerte.

III

Un ser—indivisible—yace, nulo,
Muerto, del todo muerto, todo muerto.
La evidencia deslumbra, sobrecoge,
Me arrebata la fe que era esperanza,
Esperanza en la magia prometida.
Heme aquí frente al muerto irresistible
Que revela, tranquilo, su verdad.

This Dead Man

Psyche. The most
Delicate, transparent butterfly.
Less: the transparency
Of air, without visible substance.
Perhaps the aroma
Of a wilting flower.
Am I an immortal fragrance?

II

Life is life. Ay! Death is death.

III

A being—indivisible— lies null
And dead, completely dead, all dead.
The evidence bewilders and surprises,
Wrenches from me the faith that was once hope,
Hope in a promised magic.
I stand before the irresistible dead man.
At peace at last, he tells me his truth.

A este poema se añade, a la sombra goethiana, este com-
plemento:

To this can be added, in Goethe's shadow, a complementary poem:

Hacia el hombre

Man sehnt sich nach des Lebens Bächen,
Ach! nach des Lebens Quelle hin.—*Faust*, I, STUDIERZIMMER

Si dioses ya no esperan tras la tumba,
¿Nuestra muerte despoja de sentido
Final a nuestra vida y su torrente?

Que el esfuerzo domine tal balumba.
Lanzar me baste al curso del olvido
La intención de ser hombre dignamente.

Toward Man

Man sehnt sich nach des Lebens Bächen,
Ach! nach des Lebens Quelle hin. —*Faust*, I, STUDIERZIMMER

If gods no longer wait beyond the tomb
Then are the torrents of this life despoiled
By death of any final sense?

May we throw off the burden of this gloom.
Suffice it for me to cast into oblivion's
Career the wish for human dignity upheld.

«Dignamente» está dicho aquí con toda humildad. El autor de *Aire Nuestro* conserva de su infancia el fondo cristiano, al que nunca se ha sentido ajeno. Y aquella moral se ha transformado en sentimientos, profundos e irrenunciables sentimientos. A *Homenaje* pertenece «El agnóstico». En *Y Otros Poemas* se comentan así aquellos versos:

"Human dignity upheld" is said here in all humility. The author of *Aire Nuestro* retains from his childhood a Christian formation, from which he has never felt estranged. And that Christian moral sense has been transformed into deep feelings which cannot be renounced. "The Agnostic" belongs to *Homenaje*. In *And Other Poems* it is glossed thus:

«El agnóstico»

La fe de aquella infancia tan lejana
Quedó allá, bien sepulta bajo el tiempo.
¿Qué fue de aquellos mitos con sus ritos?
¿Pereció todo? No.
                          Profundamente
Subsisten vivacísimas palabras
Donde laten perennes sentimientos.
El amor y la paz, hermanos todos,
La piedad, la humildad.
                          ¿Somos hermanos?
Gran paradoja siempre extraordinaria.

"The Agnostic"

The faith of that far-removed childhood
Stayed there, buried deep in time.
What happened to those myths and rites?
Did all that perish? No.
                          In the depths,
The liveliest words survive
Where undying feelings beat.
Love and peace, brothers all,
Compassion and humility.
                          Are we brothers?
Great paradox, ever extraordinary.

La fe de aquella infancia tan lejana . . . Hay un poema no corto, «Pietá», sobre la compasión. Y otro poema análogo sobre la humildad: «Dimisión de Sancho». (Los dos textos en «A la altura de las circunstancias».) Estos temas no son la base de una moral abstracta sino de profundos sentimientos, de un modo de ser. Por eso dice Croce que no podemos no ser cristianos en el sentido moral de esa palabra. El hombre de Occidente, por destino histórico, ve el cristianismo desde dentro, no desde fuera. Y de ahí, también, el sentimiento de la Creación. Esa Creación universal se intuye mejor de noche. Veamos «Al margen de Novalis» en *Homenaje*:

The faith of that far-removed childhood. . . . There is a rather long poem, "Pietá," about compassion. And another analogous poem on humility: "Dimisión de Sancho" ("Sancho's Surrender"). (Both of them in "At the Height of Circumstances.") These themes are not the basis of an abstract moral system, but of profound feelings, of a way of being. This is why Croce says that we cannot not be Christian in the moral sense of the word. Western man, by historical destiny, sees Christianity from within, not from without. And thence, also, the sentiment of Creation. Universal Creation is sensed best at night. Let's look at "Intimate, Alien Night," from "In the Margin of Novalis" (*Homenaje*):

Noche nuestra, noche ajena

Zu der heiligen, unaussprechlichen
Geheimnisvollen Nacht—Hymnen an die Nacht, I

¡Oh noche pura bajo las estrellas!
Firme y sereno cielo me ilumina
Sin romper esta dulce oscuridad
Que me oculta amparándome. Los hombres,
Invisibles los unos a los otros,
Ven compañía en las constelaciones,
Que tiemblan sólo si las contemplamos
A través de una atmósfera cruzada
Por nuestras inquietudes. Noche pura,
A los ojos clemente aunque terrible
Por espacios y espacios remotísimos
En unas soledades tan vacías
Mientras no las alumbre una conciencia,
Una mirada de atención amante.
Dentro de este sosiego—que mantengo
Yo también a compás de tantos astros—
Se alza la noche donde todos somos
Solos y juntos una incomprensible
Trabazón soberana de minúsculos.
Eterno es Dios o el universo. ¡Noche!

Intimate, Alien Night

Zu der heiligen, unaussprechlichen
Geheimnisvollen Nacht—Hymnen an die Nacht, 1

Oh night, pure night beneath the stars!
The firm, serene heavens illumine me
But without breaking this sweet dark
That conceals and shelters me.
Invisible to each other, men
Yet see company in the constellations,
Which tremble only if we contemplate them
Through an atmosphere criss-crossed
With our own uneasy worries. Pure night,
So clement to the eye, though terrible
Across spaces, the far remotest spaces
In solitudes so empty—
As long as consciousness, the glance of a quick
Attention, does not enlighten them.
And within this calm—which I too maintain
To the rhythm of the multitude of planets—
The night arises where we all,
Alone and yet united, form
An incomprehensible sovereign
League of the tiny.
God or the universe, eternal. Night!

En la noche, el universo. Y ahí, el hombre, en su trayectoria colectiva y personal de la vida a la muerte. Hay casos en que el sujeto de esa trayectoria, si es artista, deja algo: su expresión. Tema final: la poesía como asunto de la poesía: un poema extenso en *Cántico*: «Vida extrema». Para ese tipo de hombres, la vida no se acaba de vivir si no se expresa. La expresión no es un agregado superfluo. Es la última etapa del ciclo vital. Ese impulso primero «se muda en creación . . . Gracia de vida extrema, poesía». En *Homenaje* una sección se llama «Tiempo de leer, tiempo de escribir». En el último libro, una larga serie se desarrolla bajo el título «Res poética», lo que no se parece al *Ars Poetica* de Horacio. No arranca de una doctrina sino de una experiencia que desemboca en esas expresiones. No se formula un sistema. —¿Es usted surrealista?— Se trata de lo que se va conociendo como hacedor de poemas. De *Cántico* es el soneto:

The universe at night. And there, man, in his collective and individual passage, from life to death. There are cases in which he who follows that trajectory, if an artist, expresses something and leaves it behind him. A final theme: poetry itself as the subject of poetry—a long poem in *Cántico*: "Vida extrema" ("Extreme Life"). For this person, life is not lived fully if it is not expressed. Expression is not something superfluous, merely added on. It is the final stage of the vital cycle. This impulse first "becomes creation. . . . The grace of life lived to the extreme, poetry." In *Homenaje*, one section is called "Time to Read, Time to Write." In the latest book, a long series is developed under the title "Res poética," which does not really resemble Horace's *Ars Poetica*. It derives not from a doctrine, but rather from experiences which culminate in these expressions. It is not the formulation of a system: Are you a Surrealist? It's a matter of what one learns as a maker of poems. From *Cántico*, the sonnet:

Hacia el poema

Porque mi corazón de trovar non se quita—JUAN RUIZ

Siento que un ritmo se me desenlaza
De este barullo en que sin meta vago,
Y entregándome todo al nuevo halago
Doy con la claridad de una terraza,

Donde es mi guía quien ahora traza
Límpido el orden en que me deshago
Del murmullo y su duende, más aciago
Que el gran silencio bajo la amenaza.

Se me juntan a flor de tanto obseso
Mal soñar las palabras decididas
A iluminarse en vívido volumen.

El son me da un perfil de carne y hueso.
La forma se me vuelve salvavidas.
Hacia una luz mis penas se consumen.

Toward the Poem

Porque mi corazón de trovar non se quita—JUAN RUIZ

From the hubbub in which I wander, lost,
A rhythm disentangles itself for me,
And yielding wholly to this new allure,
I come upon the clarity of the terrace—

My guide here is the one who with clear strokes
Traces the coherence that lets me free
Myself from the goblin of disorder, so much
More melancholy than the threat of silence.

At the height of this obsessive reverie
The words, determined now to come to light,
Converge for me in a bright totality.

The sounds give me the sketch of flesh and bone.
The life-preserving boon that saves me is the form.
My pains, my sorrows, throw themselves into the flame.

Se pasa, pues, de un caos interior, de una confusión apenas pensada, apenas pronunciada, a una iluminación, esa «terraza» donde se consigue un ritmo, un orden, una forma. Sin forma estaríamos perdidos. Forma que quiere decir algo, no abstracta, sí figura viva: «El son me da un perfil de carne y hueso», y asoma ya un mundo. No se juega con signos, como creen algunos, que sólo significan signos, con lenguaje que sólo significa lenguaje. Este lenguaje, no hay duda, alude a una realidad, posee un significado que trasciende la palabra.

Hay también en este grupo textos que se refieren a los varios incidentes de la vida literaria. Importa la relación con el lector, con el crítico. El poeta de *Aire Nuestro* se dirige siempre, desde la soledad de su pluma, a un lector. Sin él no se llegaría a realizar el acto literario. He aquí:

One moves, then, from an inner chaos, from a confusion—scarcely thought, scarcely articulated—to an illumination: that "terrace" where a rhythm, an order, a form is found. Without form, we would be lost. Form that means something, not abstract form, but a living figure: "The sounds give me the sketch of flesh and bone," and a world appears. It is not a play of signs, as some believe, that signify only signs, of language that signifies only language. This language, and about this there can be no doubt, refers to a reality, it has a meaning that transcends the word.

Also in this group there are texts that refer to various incidents of literary life. The relationship with the reader and with the critic is important. The poet of *Aire Nuestro* always addresses, from the solitude of his pen, a reader, without whom the literary act is incomplete. Here we have:

De lector en lector

Pour qui écrit-on?—SARTRE

Con el esteta no invoco
«A la inmensa minoría»,
Ni llamo con el ingenuo
«A la inmensa mayoría».
Mi pluma sobre el papel
Tiene ante sí compañía.

Me dirijo a ti, lector,
Hombre con toda tu hombría,
Que sabes leer y lees
A tus horas poesía.
Buena para ti la suerte.
¡Si fuese buena la mía!

Yo como el diestro en la plaza
Brindo.
      «Brindo por usía
Y
Por toda la compañía»
Posible.

From Reader to Reader

Pour qui écrit-on?—SARTRE

I do not appeal, with the esthete,
"To the immense minority."
Nor, with the ingenuous, do I call
"To the immense majority."
My pen on the paper
Has before it all its company.
Reader, I turn to you,
A man in all your humanity,
You who can read, and do read
In your leisure, poetry.
Your lot is fortunate.
If only I had such prosperity!

Like the master in the bull ring
I make an offering.
                    "I hail your excellency
And
All the company"
Possible.

«La inmensa minoría», fórmula de Juan Ramón. «La inmensa mayoría», de Blas de Otero. (Excelente poeta, cuya obra abunda en alusiones de historia literaria. Sin conexión con la inmensa mayoría.)

Otro poema de esta sección:

"The immense minority," Juan Ramón's formula. "The immense majority," Blas de Otero's.[18] (A fine poet, whose work abounds in allusions to literary history—no connection with the immense majority.)

Another poem from that section:

Orden cronológico

Porque el poema es cosa de poscepto, y el
dogma cosa de precepto—UNAMUNO

«Se debe escribir así.»
¡Sí, sí!
Hable el crítico después
De escrita—¿cómo?—la obra,
No al revés,
Porque su consejo sobra.
No se impaciente: después.

¡Es tan vano
Poner al «infractor» multas
De antemano!

Crítico: tu fuerza abultas.
En el lenguaje más llano
Me reúno
Con don Miguel de Unamuno:
Estemos a las resultas.

Digamos con el francés:
¿La charrue devant les bœufs?
¿Orden ni en tiempo ni espacio?
Después, crítico, después
Y despacio.

Chronological Order

Porque el poema es cosa de poscepto,
y el dogma cosa de precepto. —UNAMUNO

"One should write this way."
Yes, yes!
But let the critic speak afterward,
When the work is done (and how, did you say?),
Not before—it's absurd!—
For his counsel's superfluous.
Sit still! Afterward.

It's pointless
To punish the "offender's" sins
Before he begins!

Critic: you strike a muscular pose?
In words far from difficult
I would echo the advice
That was Don Miguel de Unamuno's:
Let's check the result.

And as the French put it: The
"Charrue devant les bœufs?"
No Order, neither in time nor space?
Afterward, critic, afterward—
And without haste.

¿El crítico sugiere al autor cómo tiene que escribir? ¿Y cómo lo sabe el crítico si el autor no lo sabe tampoco? «Estemos a las resultas». Expresión por completo burocrática.

Y llegamos al fin de *Aire Nuestro*: «Remate». El fin del fin. Aquí, el «Resumen».

Can the critic tell the author how to write? And how can he know, when the author himself doesn't even know? "Let's check the result." A thoroughly bureaucratic expression.

With that we arrive at the end of *Aire Nuestro*: "Remate" ("Finishing touch"). The end of the end. And here, the "Summary."

Resumen

Me moriré, lo sé, Quevedo insoportable,
  No me tiendas eléctrico tu cable.

Amé, gocé, sufrí, compuse. Más no pido.
  En suma: que me quiten lo vivido.

Summary

I will die, I know, unbearable Quevedo.
   Don't try to sweep me up in your tornado.

I loved, joyed, suffered, wrote. I ask no more than this.
   In sum: Let them try to take back what I've lived.

«Que me quiten lo vivido» corresponde a la frase de la lengua: «que me quiten lo bailado». El autor advierte que admira mucho a Quevedo, escritor formidable. Pero disiente de su doctrina. En *Y Otros Poemas* hay un poema de dos páginas, gran elogio de Quevedo: «Última cima / De visión, de invención, de triunfo y calma».

¿Cuál podría ser el último poema leído de *Aire Nuestro*? Casi el último de la obra: «El cuento de nunca acabar». Lo cuenta un protagonista ya anciano. «El mar, el cielo», o sea, la Creación, «bajo luz serenadora». (Y, sin embargo . . . El poema está dedicado al hijo del autor. Comentó Claudio: «Es muy triste».) Estos versos, un poco testamentarios, procuran infundir serenidad. «Un abierto balcón, / Una sombra latente junto al muro / De una calle . . .» Recuerdo de Andalucía, la calle, cal blanca. Entre las infinitas creaciones valiosas del hombre, sorprende aún al hablante como la maravilla de las maravillas, «Por entre los desórdenes innúmeros, / La habitual maravilla de una orquesta». Ese es el fondo de *Aire Nuestro*: el caos y su posible superación, el desorden y el orden inicial o final; *Cántico* y *Clamor*. Y, por fin, *Homenaje*. Así «La Cumbre», de *Y Otros Poemas*. «¿Alguna especie de milagrería? / ¿Suceso que tal vez tan sólo ocurre? / Escuchad bien, mirad. Es una orquesta». Algo se puede hacer en este mundo terrenal. «El ser es el valor». Y la palabra que lo expresa. Finalmente, «Tierra bajo mis plantas, / El mar y el cielo con nosotros, juntos». El hombre en su relación con su planeta. ¿Un cuento que no se acaba nunca?

"Let them try to take back what I've lived" corresponds to the expression "Let them try to take back what I've danced." The author hastens to point out that he greatly admires Quevedo, a remarkable writer. But he disagrees with his doctrine. *And Other Poems* includes a two-page poem in great praise of Quevedo: "The highest peak / Of vision, of invention, of triumph and calm."

What could be the last poem read from *Aire Nuestro?* Almost the last one in the book: "A Never-Ending Tale." It is told by an old man. "Sea and sky," that is, Creation, "beneath the clearing light." (And yet. . . . The poem is dedicated to the author's son, Claudio, who said: "It's very sad.") These verses, somewhat like a poetic testament, try to inspire serenity in the reader. "An open balcony, / A hidden shadow by the wall / Along a street." A memory of Andalusia, narrow streets, whitewash. And among man's many worthy creations, the poet still finds astonishing, wonder of wonders, "Among innumerable convulsive troubles, / The everyday miracle of an orchestra." This is at the root of *Aire Nuestro:* Chaos and the possibility of overcoming it, disorder and the initial or final order: *Cántico* and *Clamor.* And, finally, *Homenaje.* Thus the poem, "La cumbre" ("The Peak"), from *And Other Poems.* "Some kind of sorcery? / Something that just happens? / Listen well, look. It is an orchestra." Something *can* be done on this earthly world. "Being is what counts." And the word that expresses it. Finally, "Earth beneath my feet, / Sea and sky with us, together." Man in relation to his planet. A story that never ends?

El cuento de nunca acabar

A mi hijo

El mar, el cielo, fuerzas sin fatiga,
Concurren bajo luz serenadora.
Sólo soy yo en la tarde el fatigado.

Se impone a todos este azul intenso,
Azul tendido hacia su propia calma,
Apenas iniciándose
Variaciones de espuma.
Vagos cuerpos de nubes
Aguardan el crepúsculo y su fiesta.
Mis ojos ven lo que han amado siempre,
Y la visión seduce más ahora,
Frágil bajo penumbras
Que a través, ay, de esta mirada mía
Tienden hacia lo umbrío.
Los años, si me dieron sus riquezas,
Amontonan sus números,
Y siento más veloz
La corriente que fluye arrebatándome
De prisa hacia un final.

No importa. La luz cuenta,
Nos cuenta sin cesar una aventura,
Y no acaba, no acaba:
Desenlace no hay.
Aventura de un sol y de unos hombres.
Todos, al fin extintos,
Se pierden bajo un cielo que los cubre.
El cielo es inmortal.
Feliz quien pasa aquí,
Si este planeta le ha caído en suerte,

A Never-Ending Tale

To my son

Sea and sky, indefatigable powers,
Concur beneath the clearing light.
Only I, in the afternoon, am weary.

This intense blue imposes itself on all,
A blue arched toward its own calm,
Just beginning to form
Variations of the sea-spray.
Vague-bodied clouds
Await the festival of twilight.
My eyes scan what they have always loved,
A vision even more seductive now,
Fragile beneath the shadows
That lean across my gaze toward darkness.
If the years have given me their riches
Yet they pile up their numbers
And the current that carries me
Hurriedly toward my end
Seems swifter.

It does not matter. The light counts,
Ceaselessly recounts an adventure,
And does not end, does not end:
There is no conclusion.
The adventure of a sun and some men.
Extinguished finally,
Lost as a sky closes over them.
The sky is immortal.
He is happy to whom it has fallen
To spend his ephemeral days—

Sus efímeros días
Como los del follaje
Que será amarillento.
¿Soy yo más que una hoja
De un árbol rumoroso?
Un destino común
—¿El único?—nos junta en la corteza
De un astro siempre activo,
Todos así partícipes
De un movimiento que conduce a todos
Hacia . . . ¿Tal vez no hay meta?

Ese mundo, que en mí se va perdiendo,
Frente a mí sigue intacto
Con su frescor de fábula.

Un abierto balcón,
Una sombra latente junto al muro
De una calle en la siesta del estío,
Calles, ciudades, campos, cielos, luces
Infinitas . . . Y el hombre
Con su poder terrible,
Y en medio de los ruidos,
Por entre los desórdenes innúmeros,
La habitual maravilla de una orquesta.

Una vida no cabe en la memoria.

Ámbitos de amistades,
Espíritus sin roce
Con Historia, con público,
La mujer, el amor, las criaturas,
Nuestra existencia en pleno consumada
Entre bienes y males.

Like those of the yellowing leaves—
On this planet.
Am I more than a leaf
On a rustling tree?
A common destiny—
The only one?—unites us on the crust
Of a planet always astir,
All of us caught up
In the motion that leads us
Toward. . . . Is there perhaps no purpose?

The world which in me is waning
Continues before me, intact
In its cool, fabulous air.

An open balcony,
A hidden shadow by the wall
Along a street, in a summer doze,
Streets, cities, fields, skies, infinite
Lights. . . . And man
With his terrible power,
And in the midst of the din,
Among innumerable convulsive troubles,
The everyday miracle of an orchestra.

Memory cannot contain even one life.

Circles of friendships,
Spirits who do not touch
History, or public,
Woman, love, children,
Our existence consummated fully
Among good and evil.

Surge una gratitud
¿En cuántas direcciones?
Se despliega la rosa de los vientos.

¡Amigos! Este Globo
Florece bajo diálogos:
Extraordinaria flora
—Mezclándose a la selva
Que nunca se destruye—
Por entre las historias diminutas
Que recatan sin fechas los instantes
Supremos, tan humildes.
La raíz de mi ser los ha guardado
Para abocar al que yo soy. Más rico,
Respirando agradezco.
El hombre entre los hombres,
El sol entre los astros,
¿En torno a una Conciencia?

(Más que una hoja yo no soy, no sé.)

Miro atrás. ¡El olvido me ha borrado
Tanto de lo que fui!
La memoria me oculta sus tesoros.
¿Cómo decir adiós,
Final adiós al mundo?
Y nadie se despide de sí mismo,
A no ser en teatro de suicida.
Estar muerto no es nada.
Morir es sólo triste.
Me dolerá dejaros a vosotros,
Los que aquí seguiréis,
Y no participar de vuestra vida.
El cuento no se acaba.
Sólo se acaba quien os cuenta el cuento.

In how many directions
Does gratitude spill?
The compass rose unfolds.

Friends! This Globe
Flourishes with dialogues:
Extraordinary flora
(Mingling with the jungle
That is never destroyed)
Among the diminutive histories
That preserve without dates
Those supreme, most humble, instants.
The root of my being has kept them
To form the one I am. Richer,
Full of breath, I give thanks.
Man among men,
Sun among stars—
Spinning round some Consciousness?

(Am I more than one leaf, I don't know.)

I look back. Oblivion has blurred
So much of what I was!
Memory conceals its treasures.
How can one say good-bye,
A final good-bye, to the world?
And no one takes leave of himself,
Except in the drama of suicide.
Being dead is nothing.
Dying is merely sad.
It will grieve me to leave you—
You who will go on here—
And to have no part in your life.
The tale does not end.
Only he who tells you the tale comes to an end.

¿Habrá un debe y haber
Que resuma el valor de la existencia,
Es posible un numérico balance?
Ser, vivir, absolutos,
Sacros entre dos nadas, dos vacíos.
El ser es el valor. Yo soy valiendo,
Yo vivo. ¡Todavía!
Tierra bajo mis plantas,
El mar y el cielo con nosotros, juntos.

Will there be a reckoning of debit and credit
To sum the worth of existence?
Is there some numerical balance?
Absolute being, and living,
Sacred between the two nothings, two voids.
Being is what counts. I amount to something,
I am alive. Still!
Earth beneath my feet,
Sea and sky with us, together.

Notes and Appendices

Notes

1. *Décima*. A verse form much favored by Guillén; it consists of ten octosyllabic lines rhymed *ababccdeed*.

2. *Romance*. A poetic composition of any number of lines, the even-numbered verses rhymed (generally in assonance), the odd-numbered ones unrhymed. The great body of sixteenth- and seventeenth-century Spanish balladry is composed of *romances*, and it is a meter commonly used to our day.

3. Jorge Manrique (1440?-1479). Author of "Coplas por la muerte de su padre" ("Verses on the Death of his Father"), perhaps the most famous Spanish elegy, of great influence on later Spanish poetry.

4. Rubén Darío (1867-1916). Nicaraguan poet who revolutionized poetry written in Spanish, giving impetus to *modernismo*, a movement which assimilated influences of the French Parnassian and Symbolist schools.

5. Luis de Góngora y Argote (1561-1627). Principal poet of the *culteranista* school, scorned from his time to ours for the supposed obscurity of his poetry in such compositions as the *Soledades* and *La fábula de Polifemo y Galatea*. The Generation of 1927 rescued his work from traditional excoriation.

6. Juan Ruiz, the Archpriest of Hita (1283?-1351?). Author of the *Libro de buen amor* (*Book of Good Love*), today the most widely read work of the Spanish Middle Ages, noted for its spontaneous tone and use of popular and quasi-popular elements.

7. Fray Luis de León (1528-1591). Augustinian friar, humanist, and professor of Theology at the University of Salamanca. His poetry is noted for its serenity and contemplative detachment. His characteristic metric form was the *lira*, a five-line stanza which alternates verses of seven and eleven syllables.

8. Miguel Hernández (1910-1942). Self-taught poet of humble origins, his first book of verse *Perito en lunas* (1933, *Expert on Moons*), established his fame as a neo-Gongorist poet, and won him the favor of Guillén and his group. During the Spanish Civil War he fought on the Republican side and turned his art to that cause, writing poetry as well as theater intended to be recited at the front. He died of tuberculosis in a Fascist prison.

9. Juan Ramón Jiménez (1881-1958). The Spanish poet who inherited Rubén Darío's mantle and continued writing in the *modernista* style until the publication of *Diario de un poeta recién casado* (1917,

Diary of a Recently Married Poet), from which time he practiced a "pure poetry." Jiménez' encouragement of the young poets, and the example of his relentless search for the "exact word," was of great influence on Guillén's generation. Jiménez received the Nobel Prize for Literature in 1956.

10. José Ortega y Gasset (1883-1955). Essayist and philosopher whose articles and books—particularly *España invertebrada* (1921, *Invertebrate Spain*), *El tema de nuestro tiempo* (1923, *The Theme of Our Time*), *La deshumanización del arte* (1925, *The Dehumanization of Art*) and *La rebelión de las masas* (1929-30, *The Revolt of the Masses*)—were largely responsible for forming the aesthetic and ethical tastes of the Spain of his time. He founded and directed the *Revista de Occidente* (1923-1936, generally held to be one of the finest intellectual and cultural reviews in Europe in those years), in which Ortega published much of the work of the young poets of 1927.

11. Silvio Pellico (1789-1845). Italian patriot and romantic dramatist, imprisoned for his association with the *Carbonari*. Guillén alludes here to *Le mie prigioni* (1832, *My Prisons*), which records the spiritual crisis he suffered during his eight years in prison.

12. Carlos Arniches (1866-1943). Playwright and author of numerous *sainetes* (short skits) to which Guillén refers here. The early *sainetes* deal humorously with low-life Madrid, but in the twenties Arniches introduced a note of social criticism into his theater.

13. Pedro Salinas (1891-1951). Poet, critic, and playwright of the Generation of 1927. His poetry written before the civil war— *Presagios* (1923, *Presages*), *Seguro azar* (1929, *Certain Chance*), *Fábula y signo* (1931, *Fable and Sign*), *Razón de amor* (1936, *Reason of Love*)— often reflects a verbal playfulness and celebrates elements of a modern industrial society, the legacy of earlier avant-garde movements. Yet, like Guillén's poetry, it is unified by language and intent: particularly in its treatment of the contrast between appearance and reality.

14. *Libro de miseria de omne*, *Libro de buen amor* (see note 6, above), *Las coplas de Mingo Revulgo*. Medieval satirical works, didactic in intent, critical of Spanish society of their day.

15. A famous line from Manrique's "Coplas . . ." (see note 3, above).

16. "Epístola moral a Fabio" ("Moral Epistle to Fabio"). This long anonymous poem of the seventeenth century, attributed to Fernández de Andrade, among others, is celebrated as much for its clarity and serenity of form and thought as for its expression of a Senecan and Horatian Stoic attitude.

17. Francisco Gómez de Quevedo y Villegas (1580-1645). Poet and satirist, Quevedo was a master of *conceptismo*, a mode of Spanish Baroque poetry that takes its name from its preference for elaborate metaphysical conceits. Quevedo was an archenemy of the *culteranistas*; and Góngora, principal among them, often became the target of his satirical barbs. Guillén refers here to the Christian Stoicism that informs much of Quevedo's work.

18. Blas de Otero (1916-   ). Perhaps the finest poet of the generation immediately following the civil war. Otero's earliest work (which he has since repudiated) was religious. He soon took up social themes, and has turned his art to the "immense majority," Spain's oppressed working class.

Jorge Guillén

1893:   Born 18 January in Valladolid.

1903-1909: Secondary schooling at the Instituto de Valladolid.

1909-1911: Resident at the Maison Perreyve of the French Fathers of the Oratory, in Fribourg, Switzerland.

1911-1913: Student of Philosophy and Letters at the University of Madrid; resident of the Residencia de Estudiantes, in Madrid.

1913:   September: Awarded the *Licenciatura en Letras* (Master of Arts) by the University of Granada.

1913-1914: Lives in Halle and Munich, Germany.

1914-1917: Lives in Madrid and Valladolid.

1917-1923: "Lecteur d'Espagnol" at the Sorbonne, Paris.

1918:   Paris; composes first poems.

1919:   *Cántico* conceived and begun in Brittany (Tregastel) during the summer.

1921:   17 October: married to Germaine Cahen.

1922:   28 December: daughter Teresa born in Paris.

1923:   17 September: death of mother in Valladolid.

1924:   Granted degree of *Doctor en Letras* by the University of Madrid.

            2 September: birth of son Claudio in Paris.

1925:   Passes *oposiciones* (examinations) in Madrid for professorship in Spanish Language and Literature.

1926-1929: Professor of Spanish Literature at the University of Murcia.

1928:   First edition of *Cántico* (Madrid, Revista de Occidente).

1929-1931: Lecturer in Spanish at Oxford University.

1931-1938: Professor at the University of Seville.

1936:   September: jailed as a political prisoner in Pamplona. Second edition of *Cántico* (Madrid, Cruz y Raya).

1938:   Leaves Spain.

1938-1939: Professor at Middlebury College, Vermont.

1939-1940: Professor at McGill University, Canada.

1940-1958: Professor at Wellesley College, Massachusetts.

1945:   Third edition of *Cántico* (Mexico, Litoral).

1947:   Visiting Professor at Yale University. 23 October: death of wife Germaine in Paris.

1949:   Summer in Valladolid. Begins *Clamor*.
1950:   1 April: death of father in Valladolid.
           September-December: Visiting Professor at the Colegio
               de México (Mexico City).
           Fourth edition (first complete) of *Cántico* (Buenos Aires,
               Sudamericana).
1951:   Visiting Professor at the University of California, Berke-
               ley.
1952-1953: Visiting Professor at Ohio State University.
1954:   Summer in Italy.
           Awarded Guggenheim Fellowship.
1955:   In France, Menorca, Italy.
           Receives Award of Merit of the American Academy of
               Arts and Letters.
1957:   Poetry Prize of the City of Florence.
           Maremágnum (*Clamor*, I) published (Buenos Aires,
               Sudamericana).
1957-1958: Charles Eliot Norton Professor of Poetry at Harvard
               University.
1958:   Emeritus, Wellesley College.
1958-1959: Travels in Greece, Spain, France, Italy.
1959:   Awarded the Etna-Taormina Poetry Prize, Sicily.
1960:   Travel and residence in the United States, Puerto Rico,
               Italy.
           . . . *Que van a dar en la mar* (*Clamor*, II) published (Buenos
               Aires, Sudamericana).
1961:   Grand Prix International de Poésie, V Biennale de
               Knokke-Le Zoute, Belgium.
           August-November: Visiting Professor at the University
               of the Andes, Bogotá, Columbia.
           11 October: married to Irene Mochi-Sismondi in
               Bogotá. *Language and Poetry* (expanded version of the
               Norton Lectures) published (Cambridge, Harvard
               University Press).
1962:   Visiting Professor at the University of Puerto Rico.
1963:   Italy and the United States.
           A la altura de las circunstancias (*Clamor*, III) published
               (Buenos Aires, Sudamericana).
1964:   San Luca Prize, Florence.
           Visiting Professor at the University of Puerto Rico.
1966:   Visiting Professor at the University of Pittsburg.
1967:   *Homenaje* published (Milan, Scheiwiller)

214

1968:   Visiting Professor at the University of California, San Diego.

          Aire nuestro published (Milan, Scheiwiller).

1970:   Visiting Professor at the University of Puerto Rico, Río Piedras.

          Resident in La Jolla, California and Cambridge, Massachusetts.

1971:   Summer in Paris.

1973:   *Y otros poemas* published (Buenos Aires, Muchnik).

1975:   Bennett Prize for Poetry, *Hudson Review*, New York.

1976:   Premio Miguel de Cervantes, Madrid.

1977:   Resident in Málaga.

          Premio Internazionale Fetrinelli, Accademia dei Lincei, Roma.

Main Works of Jorge Guillén

Cántico
>First edition, 75 poems (Madrid: Revista de Occidente, 1928).
>Second edition, 125 poems (Madrid: Cruz y Raya, 1936).
>Third edition, 207 poems (México: Litoral, 1945).
>Fourth edition, first complete, 334 poems (Buenos Aires: Suda-
>mericana, 1950).

Clamor, I, *Maremágnum* (Buenos Aires: Sudamericana, 1957).

Federico en persona (Buenos Aires: EMECE, 1959).

Clamor, II, . . . *Que van a dar en la mar* (Buenos Aires: Sudamericana, 1960).

Language and Poetry (Cambridge, Mass.: Harvard University Press, 1961).

El argumento de la obra (Milan: Scheiwiller, 1961).

Clamor, III, *A la altura de las circunstancias* (Buenos Aires: Sudamericana, 1963).

Cántico: A Selection, ed. by Norman Thomas di Giovanni (Boston: Little, Brown, 1965).

Homenaje (Milan: Scheiwiller, 1967).

Aire nuestro (Milan: Scheiwiller, 1968).

Affirmation: A Bilingual Anthology, trans. by Julian Palley, intro. by Jorge Guillén (Norman, Okla.: University of Oklahoma Press, 1968).

Y otros poemas (Buenos Aires: Muchnik, 1973).

Guillén also translated Valéry's *Cimetière marin*, published as *El cementerio marino* (Madrid: Alianza Editorial, 1967).

Essays in English on Guillén's work may be found in *Luminous Reality: The Poetry of Jorge Guillén*, ed. by Ivar Ivask and Juan Marichal (Norman, Okla.: University of Oklahoma Press, 1969).

Texts Used in This Reading

Aire nuestro: Cántico, Clamor, Homenaje. Milan: Scheiwiller, 1968. 1698 pp.

Y otros poemas. Buenos Aires: Muchnik, 1973. 539 pp.

Source of the Poems

35. «Hacia el hombre» *AN* (*Homenaje*), p. 1149.
36. «El agnóstico» *OP*, p. 346.
37. «Noche nuestra, noche ajena» *AN* (*Homenaje*), p. 1151.
38. «Hacia el poema» *AN* (*Cántico*), p. 273.
39. «De lector en lector» *AN* (*Homenaje*), p. 1591.
40. «Orden cronológico» *AN* (*Homenaje*), p. 1585.
41. «Resumen» *AN* (*Homenaje*), p. 1666.
42. «El cuento de nunca acabar» *AN* (*Homenaje*), pp. 1668-1671.

LIBRARY OF CONGRESS CATALOGING IN PUBLICATION DATA

Guillén, Jorge, 1893–
    Guillén on Guillén.

    Bibliography: p.
    "Main works of Jorge Guillén": p.
    I. Gibbons, Reginald.   II.   Geist, Anthony L.,
1945–   III.   Title.
PQ6613.U5G78   861'.6'2   78-70299
ISBN 0-691-06392-3
ISBN 0-691-01356-X pbk.